"*Travels Up the Creek* is a very timely, very readable scan of Alberta's ecosystems. Lorne Fitch trains his biologist's eye on everything from cheatgrass to cutthroat trout to combat biology, and he does it with humour and insight."

—DON GAYTON, ecologist and author of *The Wheatgrass Mechanism* and *The Sky and the Patio: An Ecology of Home*

"Lorne Fitch is in league with Edward Abbey, Aldo Leopold, and Wendell Berry – an environmental trinity of gentle, angry people. He has the blood-boiling passion of Edward Abbey, the heartbreaking earnestness and profundity of Aldo Leopold, and the grounded wisdom of Wendell Berry."

—JEFFREY A. LOCKWOOD, professor of natural sciences and humanities, University of Wyoming, and author of *Locust* and *Prairie Soul*

"More than merely sending out a call for the application of science to guide our paths forward, Lorne Fitch is essentially issuing a spiritual call for open eyes, ears, and voices to insist that a better way forward can – and must – be found."

—PETER KINGSMILL, writer, publications editor for the Alberta Society of Professional Biologists, and a recipient of Canada's Governor General's Conservation Award

TRAVELS UP THE CREEK

# Travels
## *Up the*
# Creek

### A BIOLOGIST'S SEARCH FOR A PADDLE

### LORNE FITCH, P. Biol.

**RMB**

For information on purchasing bulk quantities of this book, or to obtain media excerpts or invite the author to speak at an event, please visit rmbooks.com and select the "Contact" tab.

RMB | Rocky Mountain Books Ltd.
rmbooks.com
@rmbooks
facebook.com/rmbooks

Cataloguing data available from Library and Archives Canada

ISBN 9781771607131 (softcover)
ISBN 9781771607148 (electronic)

All illustrations are by Liz Saunders unless otherwise noted.

Copy editor: Peter Enman
Proofreader: Kelly Laycock
Design: Lara Minja, Lime Design

Printed and bound in Canada

We acknowledge the financial support of the Government of Canada through the Canada Book Fund and the Canada Council for the Arts, and of the province of British Columbia through the British Columbia Arts Council and the Book Publishing Tax Credit.

DISCLAIMER

The views expressed in this book are those of the author and do not necessarily reflect those of the publishing company, its staff, or its affiliates.

We would like to take this opportunity to acknowledge the Traditional Territories upon which we live and work. In Calgary, Alberta, we acknowledge the Niitsítapi (Blackfoot) and the people of the Treaty 7 region in Southern Alberta, which includes the Siksika, the Piikuni, the Kainai, the Tsuut'ina, and the Stoney Nakoda First Nations, including Chiniki, Bearpaw, and Wesley First Nations. The City of Calgary is also home to Métis Nation of Alberta, Region III. In Victoria, British Columbia, we acknowledge the Traditional Territories of the Lkwungen (Esquimalt and Songhees), Malahat, Pacheedaht, Scia'new, T'Sou-ke, and W̱SÁNEĆ (Pauquachin, Tsartlip, Tsawout, Tseycum) peoples.

# Contents

# Introduction

*There's always room for a story that can
transport people to another place.*

—J.K. Rowling

Stories tell truths about place and the ways place can affect us. Our minds are shaped by place, as they are by our
genes. Stories are the threads that connect our intellect, locate
common ground and find the linkages between our history
and our future. Richard Kearney wrote: "Telling stories is as
basic to human beings as eating. More so, in fact, for while food
makes us live, stories are what make our lives worth living."
Maybe they can help us treasure the place where we live and
treat it kindlier.

I don't know if my words will increase ecological awareness,
change attitudes or behaviours. All I know is that writers
before me – Aldo Leopold, Stan Rowe, Wendell Berry and
Rachel Carson, all storytellers – were inspiring and motivating
(and still are). Their writing took me on a journey, one of
enlightenment, even epiphany.

For many who have not had the benefit of a course in biology
or ecology, knowledge comes piecemeal. There are many mis-
conceptions about the functions and processes of the natural

world. This is understandable since it is hard to imagine all the apparently incoherent parts with their linkages and functions.

Yes, more science is necessary, but what we also need is a common ability to look around us with more curiosity, scrutiny and understanding. Stories are the pathway, an ecological pilgrimage, paving the way between complexity and understanding.

The world needs observant, engaged and articulate spokespeople. It requires people who ask tough questions about climate change, species disappearance and transforming landscapes into fungible units rather than allowing trout and bears and wood lilies to exist. Generating a modicum of anger might be useful if it is directed at change and not just shouting at the TV.

We, in the Western world, have triumphed in the acquisition of stuff, but we remain as paupers in the understanding of the world outside our hermetically sealed doors. We fail in understanding our relationship to our environment and how to take care of it, for our own survival. We remain comfortably enclosed within the purpose-built walls of carefully constructed, wilful and selective ignorance. Tearing down those walls would be an act, not of destruction, but of letting in the light of awareness.

Stewardship doesn't work, is ineffective, when there is a reluctance to understand and accept the underpinnings of ecological science. That knowledge provides the map needed to navigate to an appropriate destination. One cannot be a steward of shared resources unless the essential pieces of ecological knowledge are agreed upon and then implemented.

We need to look up and around periodically when crowdthink happens. If we don't, we could end up like the pilot fixated on the instrument panel instead of the mountain looming in front of the airplane. "Reality is, when you get right down to it, consensual: a tribe or a society makes up its mind what it is going to see and then it sees it; delusion by plurality," observed Rob Schultheis. There is a hypnotic power to wishful group-thinking. We all want to be persuaded of the truth of what we want to see and hear, even when deep down we know it is too good to be true. That's why we periodically crash.

A friend whose opinion I respect once commented to me on my writing. He said, "Don't you write anything positive, on how we are coping, successfully, with environmental issues?" It's a valid point. Another colleague confessed he no longer lectures his students on all the environmental catastrophes for fear it will discourage them, disillusion them and create a sense of helplessness. But without a sense of how far up the creek we are, how do we set a course for a better place?

We should be scared, scared spitless in fact, of our current course. This could be an effective catalyst for change and adaptation instead of wishing for some technological miracle as our salvation. The world has lost half if its wildlife within my lifespan. I don't think my buying decisions in the supermarket will change the trend, but a massive cultural shift might. Fear may be a motivator if it leads to awareness and concern.

When we are on a cliff edge, staring into the abyss, the smart move is to step back. But stepping back is not in our nature, so we ignore or deny the abyss and criticize those who point out that we teeter on the edge of it. So it's better to be a speed bump, impeding group-think's current version of progress (or at least questioning it), than a lubricant enhancing it.

Is time running out for change, or is there lots of time to shift and adapt? One's perspective can vary, just as a sense of time depends on which side of the bathroom door you happen to be on.

Environmental issues are so numerous it seems overwhelming to decide where to start. But if we take on an issue, even an intractable one, we might see a path forward to a resolution – not a perfect one, but one that opens up discussion. It simply shines a bright light on the problem. The mind has a way of making a detour around uncomfortable truths unless it is forced to focus on them.

What will save grizzly bears, caribou, cutthroat trout and the other, non-charismatic microfauna and flora? It will be the vigilance and persistence of believers – people who will not accept the premise that we can't protect and restore populations of imperilled species and ensure others do not become imperilled.

The method for accomplishing such things will be multifaceted. But at the core it will be the connections that people feel, the empathy for a fellow wild traveller, what species indicate about the health of the world we too exist in, and the magical quality that seeing a wild creature and experiencing biodiversity in all its forms can bring.

We function at brief time scales yet have children who have to survive on the tomorrows not considered. It's easy to feel hopeless and it's hard to do something about it. You can't give up. The costs of giving up are too great, too catastrophic to consider. If a story can drag you back from the brink, deliver you to another place, startle your senses and get you to look differently at something you see every day, it might persuade you to change some aspect of your life you have a new perspective on.

If the contents of this book help educate you on environmental issues, inspire you, anger you and ultimately motivate you to act, my job is temporarily done.

# Prologue

———

*Conservation has to be learned,*
*but greed comes naturally.*

—Francis Gardner

An extraterrestrial, visiting us to see why we're so keen to leave Earth, might observe and ponder what we have done, and are planning to do, with the only home and planet we have. One can begin to imagine the report prepared and filed back to some obscure planet in Alpha Centauri:

*These beings on this small green and blue planet seem intelligent, are organized in novel ways and yet display an uncharacteristic blindness to their own survival, with their actions to overuse and overheat their planet. This is ever so evident with their desire to wrest an energy substance formed from ancient plant material, under many names such as coal, oil and gas, out of the very places where an essential liquid called water comes from. As an aside, this planet's inhabitants seem fixated on finding water elsewhere in their* galaxy but ignore and foul the stuff in their own backyards. This is perplexing.

Equally perplexing is the method of obtaining these energy substances from a topographically diverse landscape, a place of great natural beauty, with a stunning array of creatures not tamed and a pleasuring ground for many of the beings from their amalgamations called cities. I observed a migration to these other places about every five revolutions of the sun.

As an aside, these cities are crowded and noisy, with foul air and hard surfaces difficult for green life forms to thrive in. These green forms (called plants) produce a substance named oxygen, absolutely critical for all but a few life forms on this planet. Yet the major places these green forms exist seem under constant assault. The big green forms, called trees, are mowed down by immense machinery. This leaves behind lifeless areas often under a pall of dust from smaller machinery. The sole purpose of the activity seems to be to roam in circles, splashing through the very water that downstream drinkers require.

Sorry for the diversion; there are so many anomalies with this group of life forms. They have self-mobility but seldom use it. Their opposable thumbs are used primarily to transmit messages on some sort of handheld devices. They procreate prolifically but do things that disadvantage their progeny.

I will get back to the unique extraction methods for this energy substance. It involves gouging out holes in one place and then transporting that substance somewhere else for processing. Often the extraction method involves pumping something down deep holes under extreme pressure, which

*creates unruly subterranean ripples called earthquakes.
This violent underground rending introduces toxic substances
into water and may cause water supplies to become
unavailable for humans.*

*Some of it, the black stuff called coal, is then washed,
but it still stays black. Very curious, this endeavour! The
laundered coal is then given a long ride, often across the
water portion of the planet, to be burned. The burning of coal
and the other energy substances liberates the kind of gases
that rise in the atmosphere and add to the overheating the
planet is undergoing. No one connects the dots.*

*The holes and new landscapes created undergo a bit of
scraping and pushing of materials around. The pushers and
the scrapers say this is reassembling the land into its former
self. I may be missing something here, but the results look
nothing like the original and seem lifeless. Maybe when I
return in a millennium or so, I might see some positive changes.*

*Where this activity called "mining" has persisted, there
is a toxic stew of poisons that are transported downstream
in water. There are attempts to strain these substances out
of the water, mostly unsuccessfully. It seems like it would
make sense to keep these chemicals buried, because many
are inimical to life. It does not make sense for humans
to intentionally poison themselves. There seems to be a
perverse persistence in continuing the activity despite all
the evidence of the harmful effects this causes.*

*The food products that these beings require are
grown with prodigious amounts of energy substances.
Some of these substances dissipate into the air (adding
to overheating) while others leak into water, rendering it*

unsuitable for aquatic creatures to live in. These aquatic creatures (termed fish) are effective indicators of water quality, yet their loss does not seem to register as a concern. Curious!

Even though water is essential for these beings, some suggest that "jobs" (a form of indentured servitude) and making "money" (a curious set of tokens for trading) are more important than protecting the life-maintaining liquid. Their leaders are glib and mouth comforting assurances that all is well, but their actions speak differently. Why they are tolerated is unclear.

For all their ability to flatten mountains, eviscerate forests, drain rivers and eliminate grasslands, there seems to be an inability for humans to grapple with the aftermath of such endeavours. Despite their apparent big brains there is a worrying tendency to ignore consequences and avoid appropriate planning, and a failure to employ techniques to repair damage.

There is much available knowledge about what to do and what needs to be done. Perversely, this is ignored and met with skepticism and derision. It is one thing to be ignorant of essential knowledge; it is yet another to be equally senseless and suicidal in the face of it.

The inability of these humans to look forward is breathtaking. These human endeavours produce jobs and money (although rarely as many or as much as originally promised), and some last only about 25 orbits around their sun (sometimes not even that long). The aftermath, a legacy of water contamination, erosion, lost recreation, fewer wild animals and a landscape without beauty and integrity, can last in the order of 100-plus orbits.

I could go on, but after observing this place I am suffering from a condition these humans call "depression." Sometimes I was buoyed by the few voices speaking to the care and protection of intact places. But the majority don't seem to grasp limits, operate as if the planet was twice as big as it is and are intent on using up every bit of it at a rate that is breathtaking.

I would suggest these Earth creatures are not sufficiently advanced forms of life to warrant reaching out to them, as evidenced by their propensity to destroy the very things that provide life. They bear watching, since they are attempting to reach and colonize other planets. If they display the same destructive and cavalier attitude to other places that they show for planet Earth, we will have to intervene.

*Illustration by Liz Saunders*

exercise to allow a number of people to "see" the riparian land-scape through the same set of eyes.

A common language is created with this metric, and instead of arguing over what we perceive, from our own perspectives, interests and backgrounds, we can view the current state of the riparian area as what it is. If the riparian area is "broken" we can appreciate that status and start a discussion on how to "fix" it. With so much energy often expended on arguments over our differing visions, this short-circuits the emotion and concentrates on what is in the realm of the possible for positive change.

In that crowd of ranchers on the side of the stream, each clutching a little green workbook on riparian health assessment, was that bright, shiny hubcap of a belt buckle attached to the rancher last seen a year ago beating a hasty exit from the hall. He was quiet throughout the daylong training exercise. Everyone was on pins and needles waiting for the next outburst. It never came.

At the end of the day he pulled one of us aside and said he had spent a long time (almost a year) thinking about the information we had provided. This reconfirms that people need time to absorb information and understand its relevance to them. His observations, tuned a bit with our insight, had led to him to conclude changes had happened on his ranch, ones he had concern over.

Over the following months, armed with new information, he stepped up to the plate and began to implement several grazing management changes to deal with some riparian health issues. Some of those changes involved fencing, to temporarily exclude livestock to allow regeneration of balsam poplars and willow, which he realized was a valuable shelter component, useful for livestock in winter and for spring calving.

He had also seen the destructive portion of the 1995 flood and knew he had to get more of nature's glue and rebar growing on his stream banks. Most of the changes, however, were related to changing the timing of riparian grazing and setting a more conservative stocking rate, both equally useful riparian management techniques.

Ironically, a good deal of what has been learned about successful riparian management, and passed on to others, has been gleaned from ranchers who are ahead of the curve. They've provided the evidence of how to do it right. Among many lessons, we have learned it is not about applying, in rigid fashion, a cookbook prescription. What is more appropriate and accepted is explaining the principles of ecosystems and of management, then allowing people to craft a solution that meets the particular needs of their landscape and operation.

These two groups, a set of cottage owners on an aging lake and a herd of ranchers on a small foothills stream, seem poles apart, geographically, socially and economically. Yet there are some remarkable similarities. They represent a new phenomenon (or a rebirth of one) in Alberta. These are people starting to take charge of their landscape, not waiting for governments to do something. They are rebuilding not just the health of their landscapes but also the sense of their communities. The realization has sunk in that riparian health is an issue we all face.

Based on evaluations that Cows & Fish has done over several years throughout the settled portion of Alberta, we face some sobering statistics. Only a small percentage of the riparian areas inventoried were deemed "healthy," providing us with the full suite of ecological functions from which all benefits, products and services flow. The rest were either "healthy, with problems," where the signs of stress are apparent, or "unhealthy," where most ecological functions were severely impaired or lost. These results go well beyond what could be expected in the natural variation of riparian health. This affects water quality, biodiversity and agricultural sustainability, matters that touch all of us.

It's a huge job to turn this sinking riparian elephant around, but it must be done. Regardless of our backgrounds, interests or politics, we all depend on the 2 to 5 per cent of the landscape called riparian. In the work of Cows & Fish, a community will say, "We need to do it ourselves, but we need help." Cows & Fish helps people figure out how to "eat the elephant" of issues facing them – and that can change the world, one community at a time.

It begins with one bite. The first bite is awareness, giving people some elemental understanding of the landscape they live on and make a living from. Awareness is the foundation that leads to a cumulative body of knowledge, not only about the landscape but also about who to work with, what tools are available and how to monitor changes.

Embodied in the pathway to ecological health are elements of responsibility, authority, ownership and motivation. Cows & Fish doesn't "do" things for people; rather, the opportunity is created for people to do things for themselves. One farmer summed up the approach this way: "Many organizations give us lots to think about, but Cows & Fish gives us something to think *with*."

Many of our riparian landscapes have been quietly deteriorating for many decades. This won't be turned around quickly.

An encouraging sign is that the years of applying awareness and measurement of riparian areas throughout Alberta have resulted in a growing realization of the issues and a sense that action is required.

Acknowledging our mistakes represents a fundamental shift in thinking. Ensuring we don't repeat them is the potential legacy of the work Cows & Fish does.

## PUBLIC LANDS
### *Alberta's Best Idea*

Sometimes you need to be far from your mailbox to acknowledge a good idea in your own backyard. Such is the case with Alberta's public lands. Public lands are those lands vested to us, the people of Alberta. In other words, these are our lands, in shared ownership, held in trust for us by the government of the day.

That public land is a good idea became clear to me while travelling through Texas, a place where a paltry 1.5 per cent of the state is public. Imagine a jurisdiction with so little public land it hardly registers in the psyche of its citizens. In a recent issue of *Texas Monthly*, the state magazine, was an article on "75 Reasons to Love Texas." Amid BBQ, cowboys and country and western music there were only two references to use of public land, and both were for federal parks.

Large portions of Texas seem like the land Cain was willed, where a cow has to pack a lunch to cross. Why it's in private hands is history, a perplexing conundrum in today's world of expanding population, with recreational and ecological expectations to be met.

Contrast the Texas situation with Alberta, where public land is about 60 per cent of the province, private land is about 30 per cent and federally owned lands make up about 10 per cent.

Alberta and Texas are roughly the same size. If we were to follow the example of Texas related to public land, as some politicians are suggesting, we, the Alberta public, would be left with less than 10,000 square kilometres. That's not much more than the current combined size of all First Nations reserves in the province, where the burgeoning population is stretching the limits.

We don't have a Parthenon, an Acropolis or ancient palaces in Alberta. What we have is wild space, a natural heritage that has remained in public ownership and is bequeathed to us by past generations. This is an uncommon treasure, given the situation in much of the world. To say public land is part of our heritage is a point lost on some, especially those who see these lands as mere commodities, to be exploited for private or political gain. We might take pride in being Texas-sized but not in wholeheartedly embracing the Texas ideal of having all our land in private hands.

Some Albertans do propose converting the commons – public land – to private property, including libertarian politicians. The tug of war is repetitive, between those who wish to maintain public land for the public good and those who see sales as a get-rich-quick scheme. Sale of our natural heritage provides government a quick, one-time-only influx of revenue. Selling public land, a continual generator of public revenue, means Albertans lose in the end.

Alberta's public lands provide common space, particularly in densely populated central Alberta where these lands are islands in a sea of private ownership. In the grasslands, the foothills and the boreal forest, public land provides big space. In conservation of native plants and animals, big often trumps little, so the vast space afforded by public land is a bonus.

The story of the Attwater's prairie chicken is a cautionary tale about the loss of public land and the space it affords. This bird, a subspecies of the now extinct heath hen, historically ranged over the coastal plains of Louisiana and Texas by the hundreds of thousands. Now the species teeters on the edge of extinction, with about a hundred birds left in the wild.

Of the original six million acres of coastal plain that formed grouse habitat, less than 1 per cent is left. Virtually none of that is public land. Restoration efforts are stymied by the cost of acquiring private holdings and the reluctance of landowners to implement land-use changes that favour grouse.

Contrast that situation with our own imperilled bird, the greater sage-grouse. In our favour, and pivotal to restoration efforts for this Endangered species, is the vast swath of publicly owned native grasslands in southeastern Alberta, within the range of the grouse (and many more species we don't want to see disappear). If we dial back industrial disturbance, sage-grouse have a chance to thrive here again. Public lands provide Alberta a unique option for recovering the species, quickly and at low cost, one unavailable in Texas.

Instead of asking what good are public lands to Albertans, economically, ecologically and socially, we might better ask, where would we be without them? In the face of an uncertain future, we don't want to preclude options, to fail to have buffers and hedges against changes we can't yet identify. Hanging on to public lands ensures we don't sacrifice options for the future.

History shows how private ownership, even when tempered by public regulation, falls short of keeping landscapes healthy. The capitalist tendency to privatize, as the answer to a question unasked, has stumbled badly, producing degraded lands, lost opportunity and increased public costs to mitigate bad decisions.

History has locked us into a legacy of past decisions. The Canadian government, in a bid to thwart American expansion and expropriation of the west, and the Prairie provinces in particular, developed plans to dispose of great tracts of public land for settlement. This included the lands provided to railroad companies to underwrite the costs of transcontinental railway construction, a method of binding together the disparate parts of the nation.

Mostly this was successful. The exceptions included lands unsuitable for cultivation and those where inadequate rainfall precluded successful farming. The latter were taken back under the public domain as tax-recovery lands. Along the slopes of the Rocky Mountains, the forests of the Eastern Slopes were also deemed to be more important as essential watersheds, rather than in private hands for logging, mining and ranching. Much of the boreal forest was unsuitable for settlement and remained public.

The massive conversion of public land, during the homestead era and after, to private land, brought us settlement and economic progress. To a degree, those former public lands, now farmed, have given us a foundation of wealth as measured in stark ledger terms. However, the conversion of those lands also has given us declining soil fertility, increasing erosion (especially for cultivated lands), lost wetlands, degrading rivers and the transformation of landscapes with vegetative and wildlife diversity into vastly simplified ones.

Not all owners of land are rapacious, unfeeling miners of soil and vegetation or destroyers of wildlife. For many there is an ethic of stewardship, an understanding that applying the brakes, rather than continuing to accelerate pressures on the land, is beneficial. But with the exception of some minor regulatory oversight, a land ethic on the part of landowners is a personal decision. It can be shifted by economic pressures, societal leanings and successional events. Short-term economic gain often trumps long-term care. There is little or no cost, or censure, for failing to steward a piece of private land.

For users of public land for economic reasons, you abuse it at your peril. This is not to suggest all public land is free of abuse, at the hands of industry, recreationalists or leaseholders. Legislation, policy and penalties are available, waiting only for the resolve to use the instruments designed to protect these lands. Arguments can be mounted, and are, that we need to take better care of public lands, resolve land-use issues though effective planning and sort out public access to public lands. That these lands are still in the public domain enables us to have those debates.

Many of these public lands used to be labelled as "other un-improved lands," as if they were somewhat deficient, wanting or inferior. As it turns out, public lands are the greatest bargain we never really planned for. Somewhat by default, we now have this tremendous resource.

One of the virtues of public lands is that they create a bench-mark, suitable for assessing our judgment and decisions re-lated to land use. How do we know who we are, if we don't acknowledge our history? The mirror of understanding is the land, the water and the wildlife. An examination of the difference between public and private land tells us how we have treated this place called home and allows us to gauge our success at stewarding the resources of today for future generations.

Public lands may be the last frontier. In some ways what remains is an accident of history. We would be wise to view those lands as a heritage, as long as they remain public. Public ownership suggests stewardship, not exploitation, and certainly not disposal.

Wallace Stegner, no stranger to public land conversion with his Saskatchewan homestead roots, made the point: "The trouble is that places work on people very slowly, but people work on places with the single-minded ruthlessness of a beaver at a cottonwood tree." Given our continual nibbling away at the public land base in Alberta, we may not yet have evolved the societal or political maturity to understand the virtues of public land.

Public land shouldn't be viewed as a shiny bauble suitable for sale. Barring a major economic collapse, as in the 1930s with land abandonment, public land once sold is gone forever. Once you eat the cake, there's no cake left.

When 60 per cent of the province is in public ownership and, with some exceptions, available to Albertans, that empowers us as citizens, especially the 81 per cent of us who live in urban areas. It is part of our heritage, a visceral part of our societal DNA. Any government that proposes a liquidation of what is ours should be viewed as rash and heavy handed, trammelling current rights and freedoms.

Progress, real progress, is measured not solely with what we've acquired, with what we've sold, with what our economic status is, but also with what we have retained. Government, holding land in trust for the people of Alberta, needs to draw a line around public land and say, "This is public land and public land it shall stay." Public land is surely one of Alberta's best ideas — let's keep it that way.

## SAVING THE EARTH
### *Easy Steps*

———

The thing about saving the Earth — the important thing about saving the Earth — is that it isn't really about saving the Earth. The Earth is in no real danger. It is we humans who are imperilled, along with some of the attributes of the Earth we currently enjoy.

We think solutions and salvation come with more technological prowess, but what may be more important is the ability to weigh the consequences of our actions. One of the rules of physics is you can't go faster than the speed of light. This parallels what could be the first rule of human dynamics, which states you shouldn't go faster than the speed of enlightenment. The physics rule, from Einstein's special theory of relativity, is immutable. The second one is broken relatively routinely.

Like many of you I often fly on commercial airlines. I board the aircraft and dutifully snap the buckle on my seatbelt shut. I am aware of the safety briefing, which is, charitably put, a perfunctory bit of due diligence with a box ticked off somewhere in corporate headquarters that we were warned. If we don't heed the warning and read the safety card, well, it's on our heads.

None of us in these circumstances have concluded that our lives are inexorably governed by the laws of probability and confounded by chaos theory. I'm pretty sure I'll survive, based on experience and the blind faith that has most of us believing we will win the lottery but never be involved in a car accident.

All of us are passengers in a tube hurtling along, high above the landscape. Somewhere out there in those immense skies, other tubes fly filled with people, hopefully not on an intersecting course with ours. But they're on their own; they've had their own safety briefings. Some of them may be on flights that still serve meals. I try not to think of that perk.

When we all arrive safely at a destination of our choice we disembark, and all of us, from different tubes, mingle around the luggage carousel with the promise that our bags arrived too. We all make little, involuntary sighs of relief or offer silent prayers of thanks for being back on the Earth's surface.

But on the ground it isn't much different. We're still passengers on a liner hurtling through the cosmos. All the same, except there is no safety briefing. Maybe there should be a safety briefing when we return to Earth. It might make more sense than the perfunctory one we get when we climb into a tube to fly.

What could we include in that safety briefing for the planet we ride on, before we all head home, luggage safely stowed under our arms? How about:

- All of us ride this ship together; no other transport exists.
- Learn more about the craft we are riding on;
  read all the manuals.

- Consider the limited carrying capacity of this bus; don't exceed it.
- Don't lose any of the pieces; there are no replacement parts.
- If you make a mess, clean it up; otherwise, we all sit in it.
- Air, water, soil and biodiversity fuel this ship; don't screw with the fuel.
- Regular inspections and timely maintenance will keep the craft functioning.
- Share space and resources aboard the ship equitably, even with non-human passengers.
- Once on, you can't get off; it's a one-way trip.
- Keep the heat down; some parts of the craft are temperature sensitive.
- Limit your luggage; ask yourself what you really need.
- Remember, after you're gone, others will be riding on this craft; leave it nice for them.

Most importantly, it's not politicians, bureaucrats, technocrats, Christians, Muslims, Buddhists, Jews, atheists, academics, generals, farmers, loggers, plumbers, environmentalists, corporate executives, the right wingers, the left wingers or the buffalo wingers piloting this craft. It's all of us, with equal responsibility, accountability and influence.

Many of you are no doubt wondering where I'm going with this very global, very planetary, maybe even galactic line of thinking. We're now on a ride together on the third rock from the sun. Please fasten your seatbelts.

Perhaps it would be useful to start with some fundamental principles that form the "Mighty Truths" governing our approach to the world. I first heard these from a colleague, Ron

Wallace, and they are an elegant summary of what should be on a safety card for review by Earth's inhabitants. They are:

1. What goes around comes around.
2. Everything is connected.
3. Everything is additive.
4. Diversity = stability.
5. We (humans) are in the loop.

Let's explore them in a bit more detail.

"What goes around comes around" isn't just a cliché. It's an instruction manual. The world is a recycling centre on a massive scale as well as an interconnected web. We breathe the same air and drink the same water as did the dinosaurs and our ancestors. The difference is the air and water of today has been fortified with the exhausts of our industrialized world. A nuclear reactor in Japan suffers an upset and very shortly we all breathe (or drink) in the result. In the plume from multiple stacks and pipes are heavy metals, toxic chemicals and combinations whose synergistic effects are poorly understood. Once released, the substances are exported over the globe by currents that know no boundaries. This is an unintentional consequence of the global economy, that with benefits come significant costs.

"Everything is connected" speaks to the observation of John Muir, who said, "When we try to pick out anything by itself, we find it hitched to everything else in the Universe." We burn fossil fuels releasing carbon, cut down forests and rip up native prairie that store carbon, fail to invest in alternative forms of energy and then watch in amazement as polar ice caps and glaciers melt. Much of humanity is concentrated along coastlines, many of which are, or will be, subject to ocean level increases. Climate change, a consequence of the things that flow from our smokestacks and tailpipes, means weather patterns have become unpredictable and the weather vicious. Most of our agriculture, the source of our regular meals, is rain dependent. Tinker with that and your plate may not be full at suppertime.

"Everything is additive," including that second dessert or an additional drink. You may also be familiar with issues of bio-accumulation of DDT and other persistent chemicals and the effects on nesting birds and fish. Many of those substances we filter out of air, water and food with our lungs, kidneys and other organs. These things linger, accumulate and magnify in us as well, so that, as an example, mother's milk is now richly infused with persistent organic pollutants, heavy metals and endocrine-disrupting chemicals. The effects of all our endeavours are cumulative, and inevitably there is a line in the sand followed by a precipice. The science of cumulative effects analysis has progressed to provide us reasonable interpretations of overlaps, what the future trajectories are given the growth rates of today, and the signals to determine when to stop.

"Diversity equals stability" isn't just an ecological construct. Diverse systems are inherently more resilient, stable and resistant to perturbations. The principle applies to a forest, a business, to a community and to the world. I understand that to succeed in business you need to identify your assets and leverage them to create your own competitive advantage. Alberta's competitive advantage isn't solely vested in barley, beef, oil or dimensional lumber. It is our clean air, water, productive soil and biodiversity (and associated ecological goods and services) coupled with an educated and healthy population that provides our strengths. Once we lose that foundation our advantage is gone.

"We humans are in the loop." Let me incite you with something startling. Let's not kid ourselves that we manage the environment. It is impossible to send a fish on a course to swim better in less water, or a cow to a workshop on sustainable grazing or persuade water to avoid being contaminated. Less startling, but not yet fully understood, is that we are not immune from the effects of our own activities. Nothing happens in environmental management until people agree to behave in ways that recognize the effects of their actions. With recognition comes responsibility, and with responsibility eventually comes accountability. Then we will understand the challenge of living the good life without abusing the generosity of the Earth.

These five principles underpin everything. They are integrative, unifying and stand as a group to provide order to our thought processes as we try to grasp the complexity of the task. Understanding them does not mean we are granted immunity from their actions. Neither fighting the principles nor ignoring them is an option. You might be able to bargain for short-term relief, but over time, acceptance is the only option.

If saving the world and us is worthwhile, these principles form the basis for action. This may be said about maintaining our Earth – the truism that if we want a better world we will have to become better people. This is a practical, pragmatic, simple, cheap and easily adapted solution to the issues of the globe.

All that is required is changing ourselves.

## BEING A BEAVER'S LITTLE HELPER

---

Like the question of what came first, the chicken or the egg, what is the sequence of beavers and water?

Like trout, ranchers and willows, beavers need water; otherwise they can't construct dams quickly enough to dodge predators. Beavers are amazingly adaptive creatures but can't build safe homes overnight from nothing. So the answer to what needs to come first is water.

Deep water behind dams offers escape and a place from which to forage. Water is also the essential spark for woody plants like willows, aspen, cottonwoods, dogwood and other tasty morsels, also essential for dam building and maintenance.

Beavers trap and store water, mitigating floods and drought. If we want these essential ecological benefits, we need more beavers, because they are missing in action from many watersheds. Simply parachuting in beavers (as was actually done in one of the western states) is often a non-starter.

No single factor robbed watersheds of beaver. Prolonged drought periods, trapping, plus loss of riparian features like woody plants from overgrazing, logging, roads and residential development, have all taken their toll. What often remains is a stream course that might run with water for a brief time in the spring and then dries up. Sometimes it's hard to remember when such streams had perennial flow and trout swam in them, in and between beaver dams.

Without some intervention, nothing will change in these watersheds. Adaption to climate change might provide the incentive to look again at these dry creeks and ask, can we do

Restoring streams and riparian areas, to benefit trout, live-stock and downstream water drinkers, will require a partnership with beavers and a bit of a helping hand to allow them to get on with what they do so well.

## ANTELOPE
### *Icon of the Grasslands*

———

Napi, the Blackfoot trickster, is also viewed as a creator – the one who brought the land into being, the one who gave it shape and form, and the one who created the animals. Legends say that while in the mountains Napi made the antelope and turned them loose. They ran so fast they fell over some rocks and hurt themselves. Napi saw this was no place for antelope and took them down to the prairies, where they raced away with speed and grace.

This is probably the first instance of adaptive management, a process of doing, testing, changing and repeating. Adaptive management is the antithesis of doing the same thing over and over, hoping for different results. This is a topic worth returning to, on the conservation of antelope populations.

Western science tells us that like the grizzly bear, the magpie and *Tyrannosaurus rex*, the pronghorn antelope is a beast unique to western North America. Pronghorn antelope are home grown and look like they have sprung, fully formed, from the prairie grassland.

Central to antelope biology is open space. An antelope body is designed for unrestricted speed and does not fit well with forests, fences and other impediments to fast, forward trajectory. Exceptional eyesight, estimated as eight-power vision, alerts them to danger on broad prairie landscapes. They see you long before you see them. Pronghorn eyes are pools of deep, inscrutable velvet and protrude slightly from the skull, all the better to bring antelope their world – the geography of long looks.

E.C. Pielou, in *After the Ice Age*, points out that in a 3,000-year interval at the end of the Pleistocene epoch between 35 and 40 species of large mammals became extinct on the plains of North America. Two genera of pronghorn antelope, including the four-horned antelope, were part of this extinction event. This included the American cheetah, which presumably preyed on antelope.

Speedy predators like the cheetah whittled fine the fleet legs of the antelope in the great grinding wheel of natural selection. From this evolutionary interaction antelope still remember and can run faster than any current predator.

Bison, moose, elk, caribou, deer, antelope, muskoxen and mountain sheep and goat are the only grazers and browsers to survive to present times. All but antelope were immigrants from Asia. It is speculated that these species adapted to the presence of human hunters, developed wariness and escaped extinction.

Pronghorn antelope were stalked by Plains Indigenous Peoples disguised in their hides and were lured by the waving of bright cloth. Buffalo hunters and vacationing "sportsmen" used them as target practice, to fine-tune their rifles. Then meat-starved settlers nearly decimated their ranks, harvesting them by the thousands. And yet, antelope outlasted the buffalo, despite the rapacious hunters and hungry homesteaders. They were helplessly inquisitive, good to eat, amusing to shoot at

# 2

# Water: It Doesn't Require a Trip to Outer Space to Find It

*In an age when man has forgotten his origins*
*and is blind even to his most essential needs*
*for survival, water along with other resources*
*has become the victim of his indifference.*

—Rachel Carson

## WATER
### *Never a Dry Subject*

An optimist sees the glass as half full of water, the pessimist as half empty. To an engineer, the glass is twice as big as it needs to be. So there are many perspectives on water and how we manage it.

I remember a day when the rain blew sideways under leaden skies. The waitress in the coffee shop said with a dismissive sniff, "Isn't that just the way? Tomorrow's my day off and now it's ruined." The poor weather person apologizes for rain forecast for Saturday, as if they had some control over it. To minimize the feeling of inconvenience to city dwellers, some might opine that at least the rain is good for the farmers, or for ducks.

The disconnect between us and water grows wider. Rain isn't just a missed golf game, or a snow flurry an annoyance of shovelling. This is step one for a substance more precious, more useful, more perilous in supply than oil or gold or rare earths, one without which we would still be cosmic dust.

Water as an elemental substance has a recurring theme in this world and in our lives. In the fullness of time every molecule of water has been around the world and back again. Each one travelled by sea and by air and by subterranean passage, in channels and between shores. Some travelled as a passenger in an orange, an avocado or even in a human body. If water molecules could accumulate air travel miles, the rewards would be staggering.

So, the same water that dinosaurs and sabre-toothed tigers and Neanderthal man (and woman) drank, we drink today. The same water we brushed our teeth with this morning nourished the plants that formed Alberta's vast coal beds and petroleum pools. Water that transited through Genghis Khan, Charlemagne and Sitting Bull continues its endless journey through us.

At times that water is liquid. It can be harder than a frozen hockey puck. Sometimes it drapes the landscape in a soft, white covering. It can seem weightless, but visible as clouds. And, it can be invisible even to a discerning eye as vapour reaching up into the stratosphere and shielding us from solar radiation. Like a changeling, water is fluid, mobile and protean. It is a truism that thousands have lived without love, but none have lived without water.

To W.C. Fields, the thought of drinking water was anathema, because of what fish did in it. But it is still amazing stuff, this water, and perhaps it's time to stop treating it mainly as a diluent for scotch and coffee, a convenient cleanser for both body and industrial processes, a frozen platform to play our national sport on and the backdrop for tourism posters.

Water isn't a linear feature, simply passing through and by us. It is us, up to 65 per cent. The rest is just framing and wiring and plumbing. Our brains have a larger constitution of water so when we think – if we think – it's the water that is the conduit for the magic of thought.

Aldo Leopold, an ecologist and philosopher, observed that rivers are not linear but round. As metaphor he used an early logger story, one of the marvels of early Wisconsin, of the Round River, a river that flowed into itself and thus sped around and around in a never-ending circuit. Paul Bunyan, a logger of mythical proportions and of myth, discovered it and the Bunyan tale is of how he floated logs down its waters that were somehow magically connected in a never-ending circle. It's not really magic and only partially metaphor to suggest all water is like the Round River.

As part of natural cycles and rhythms, we float past our starting point endlessly, negating the thought that we are simply either upstream or downstream residents. We are in and part of a loop. Water is a circle, a cycle of energy, from sun to plants to insects to fish to us. If the circle is broken, as it is only by human activity or intervention, the entire continuum suffers, including us.

Shifts in hydrologic responses from logging, industrial development, increased nutrients from agriculture and cities, excess sediment from everything we do in the uplands, plus the loss of riparian filters, all profoundly change the linkages between the pieces that make up the connected arc. As the circle spirals out of round, out of connectedness, the pieces fall away, almost by centrifugal force. It is then hard, maybe mostly impossible, to square the water circle again.

How well we have managed water in Alberta to this point is a complex story, seen and interpreted through multiple lenses. We have, by many accounts, a healthy economy, supported by the multi-faceted use of water to irrigate, grow and process food, aid industrial development and strip tar sands of oil. Water quantity has not yet impacted urban use and growth, although some troubling signals about water quality are evident.

As cities and towns grow, the demands from a largely urban population in the province, coupled with conservation needs, will test our ability to share equitably the resource in shortest supply. We, as Albertans, might brag about swimming in oil, but the real measure of wealth is water.

There is only so much water circulating in the world and then there is no more. Sustainable systems, be they agriculture, urban, industrial or extractive, must accept and work carefully within the limits of the water cycle, it being far from an inexhaustible supply. Indeed, if there were a first commandment for living successfully and sustainably on Earth, it would be to understand how the water cycle – the Round River of Leopold's metaphor – and watersheds work together, and adapt our behaviour accordingly.

advantageous communication with the Saskashiwan River," as Jefferson hoped. So ended the expansion dreams and possible hegemony of the United States into what would become Canada.

As early settlers would develop impressions of prairie rivers, including the Milk, "they were hard to ford, destitute of fish, too dirty to bathe in, and too thick to drink." And, even more distressing, sometimes they went dry. Dawn Dickinson, long a prairie resident, related an anecdote about her mother, who had come from the green lushness of England to join her husband – a customs agent at Coutts, on the Alberta–Montana border – in the early years of the 20th century. Writing home, she described her new home this way: "It has more rivers, and less water." That was a succinct summary of the Milk River and its watershed.

As settlement of the Milk River watershed progressed, in both Alberta and Montana, the limitations of the river became evident. Tony Rees wrote in *Hope's Last Home*, "But as a pure plains river, the Milk was utterly incompatible with booster visions of an agricultural Eden along its banks because it would often deliver its spring runoff in one great flood, only to run dry in midsummer."

Prairie agricultural dreamers and schemers have always been tenacious and unwilling to accept the limitations of the landscape. Once the possible connections between the St. Mary River and the Milk headwaters were realized, the slide rules were employed to plan for the capture and diversion of mountain runoff down the Milk to thirsty Montana farms.

This probably seemed elegantly simple to the Americans, but since the St. Mary River was already tapped for irrigation in Alberta, this created a fair bit of consternation in Canada.

Canadian officials might have observed, as Jack Benny, the comedian, later wryly pointed out, "Drink Canada Dry [the soft drink] is a slogan, not a command."

It was a high-stakes poker game, maybe one of chicken, and could have resulted in the complete diversion of St. Mary River flows into the Milk. In an ultimate bluff, the Canadian reaction was to start construction of a canal, upstream of the town of Milk River, that would capture the diverted flow and direct it back north, returning the water to Canada. In time this would be called the "Spite Ditch."

The bluff worked, and this led to a more equitable water sharing agreement between the US and Canada. Later appraisals would indicate the canal may not have held water, due to extensive gravel seams. Teddy Roosevelt was the US president at the time of these negotiations, and maybe, to paraphrase his famous quote on foreign policy of "Speak softly and carry a big stick," the Canadian response was "Speak reasonably and dig a big ditch."

The water sharing agreement did not quench the thirst for water in the Milk River watershed – it just delayed future desires. In recent times, those in the Alberta portion of the Milk have lobbied hard for storage, to expand irrigation and safeguard domestic supply. However, no matter how stridently the proponents argue, there is no persuasive economic argument to be made for reservoir development. There are also engineering and ecological issues that cannot be resolved easily. The Milk River just cannot be bent to accommodate everyone's desires for water.

Except seasonally, and when enhanced by diversions from the St. Mary River, the Milk flows though a dry land, and water will always be limiting. This is apparent to us as our canoe grinds to a halt on a sandbar. A few more centimetres of water would float our boat, but we might as well ask for other miracles. Sometimes a float turns into a drag. But this is not the river's fault.

Tempering expectations of clear sailing with other virtues of the river is essential. Aridity effectively limits the human footprint. It leaves large portions of native prairie and the green zone of riparian plants alone and largely intact. Travelling on the Milk River in Alberta is a step back in time, where wild space predominates. The lower Milk River flows through a canyon of deeply dissected coulees and steep, eroded walls. Blue grama grass and cactus give way to a thin thread of cottonwoods and willows. For much of the length of the Milk River, rattlesnakes, pronghorn antelope, mule deer, ferruginous hawks, and common yellowthroats have a greater population density than do humans.

Despite periodically and seasonally drying up, except for isolated pools, remarkably the Milk River harbours 28 fish species. Three are species at risk: the St. Mary River sculpin, western silvery minnow, and stonecats. The stonecat is the only fish species in Alberta that can hurt you, outside the possibility of being lacerated by the sharp teeth of a northern pike. A poison gland at the base of the first few rays of the pectoral fin can produce a wasp-like sting if the fish is improperly handled.

All prairie creatures, aquatic and terrestrial, have come to an accommodation with aridity, water shortages and the range of variability in their environment. None of these species has unfulfilled expectations about the Milk River and its watershed. Maybe we can learn from that.

## AN EQUILIBRIUM OF MUD AND WATER

Like too much of anything – ice cream, liquor or indolence – abundant sediment, or mud, is an indicator of things gone wrong, a lack of regulatory oversight and an inability to set limits. There has always been erosion, but natural background levels of sediment in Eastern Slopes streams are low, very low. In unaffected, intact watersheds an equilibrium had developed between mud and water – mostly water, a little mud. Trout and the aquatic insects upon which they feed have adapted to that ratio over millennia.

With an excessive land-use footprint the ratio has flipped. I wonder how we would react if our relatively dirt-free drinking water got turned upside down and became mostly mud. That's what the land-use footprint has done to trout – muddied the waters, clogged the gravels and pushed them to the edge of survival.

I've spent years counting bull trout redds where the females lay their eggs in stream bed gravels. One gets an intuitive feel for where a female bull trout would like to spawn. The gravel substrate can't be too big, or too small. There must be some overhead cover in the form of a branch or log to provide some security. These elements add up to a rudimentary formula for predicting where a bull trout redd might be located.

Except my radar for detecting suitable sites has often been wrong, especially on streams like Racehorse and Dutch creeks, both with a massive logging footprint coupled with an excessive road and trail network. Despite all the right features being in place there were often no redds.

What became evident was that the gravel substrate was unyielding underfoot, like a cement sidewalk. A female bull trout would have had to evolve opposable thumbs to grasp a pick to break through this impenetrable layer.

The culprit was sediment, delivered from a watershed too busy with human activities. Sediment that is the product of weathering and erosion from sedimentary bedrock. Sediment that includes ground-up limestone – calcium carbonate or calcite – the raw material of cement. Even in its raw form, calcite is a binder that sets, hardens and adheres to stream gravels.

Spring floods generally flush sediment from the gravels, depositing most of it on the flood plain. Unfortunately, when the gravels become "cemented" there is substantial resistance to this and stream energy is diverted into a flanking movement, eroding stream banks instead. This widens stream channels and adds to the sediment burden.

This is particularly prevalent in areas of mountaintop removal, coal strip mines where calcite is liberated with overburden dumping. Carl Hunt, a retired provincial fisheries biologist, says this is now a problem in rivers receiving effluent from coal mines in the Coal Branch. It is also acknowledged by coal companies in BC as a serious issue.

The Coal Branch, in west-central Alberta, has been the epicentre for coal mining for decades. Over an 11-year period, Richard Quinlan, now a retired provincial habitat biologist, monitored impacts from five coal strip mines. In that time period there were a minimum of 22 serious incidences of sediment release, 12 of which were forwarded for charges under the federal *Fisheries Act* (but no cases went forward for prosecution).

These problems resulted from settling ponds insufficient to contain sediment-laden runoff from heavy rainfall events, and chronic levels of erosion from coal haul roads.

The epicentre for coal mines coincides with the primary distribution of Athabasca rainbow trout, Alberta's only native rainbow trout. In one case at Cardinal River Coal, heavy rainfall caused a settling pond to fail, the collapse of a mine pit and a haul road failure, resulting in the inundation of Mary Gregg Creek with sediment. Sediment filled the channel of the stream to the top of the stream banks and spilled into the riparian zone for approximately 400 metres downstream.

The impact on the Athabasca rainbow trout population was a long-term population decline affecting not just the section of stream inundated with sediment but downstream as well. It might not be surprising that these native rainbow trout are now designated as Endangered in Alberta.

Mud deposited in streams impedes trout reproduction, impacts aquatic insects, fills in pools needed for overwinter survival, can kill trout directly and also adds to stress, which increases indirect mortality. More insidiously, it can, over time, render these streams uninhabitable for trout.

In the 1970s, nine tributaries to the Wapiti River had good populations of Arctic grayling. By 2011, five streams had no grayling left, three were at low densities and only one stream retained good population levels of grayling. Adam Norris, for his master's research, looked at why populations had crashed in most of the streams.

He found a combination of logging, oil and gas development and agricultural clearing had transformed the watersheds of most of these streams. Runoff from cultivated fields brought sediment, but in addition, bonded to each sediment particle was an agrochemical stew of fertilizers, herbicides and pesticides.

Several of the streams had been transformed from relatively pristine watercourses to muddy ones with an excess of nutrients. A small increase in nutrients, especially phosphorous, promote growth and are beneficial in producing more of the things fish like to eat. Too much overwhelms the system, oxygen is robbed from the water, and beyond a phosphorus concentration threshold Arctic grayling could no longer endure.

Westslope cutthroat trout used to dominate the trout populations of the Oldman and Bow watersheds. Now they cast a mere shadow over their former distribution. Remarkably, cutthroat trout in their pure genetic form hold on in a few streams that drain the Porcupine Hills, a mostly forested chain of foothills apart from the main Eastern Slope watersheds. One stream is Beaver Creek.

Beaver Creek descends from the Forest Reserve in a narrow valley, shaded by spruce, pine and willows. It's a small stream, often no more than a metre or so wide. In the past it would murmur and clatter over gravels and cobbles. Now it muddles through deposits of sediment, largely silent and subdued.

The Beaver Creek valley has been extensively logged, first with selective harvest of Douglas fir trees. Older logging was low-impact and likely had minimal effect on the stream or the cutthroat trout population. But that style of logging was deemed uneconomical, so industrial-scale timber harvest with large clear-cuts became the norm.

Clear-cuts begat roads and roads begat a new form of recreation – one where the participants are tethered to their vehicles with an invisible umbilical cord. The purpose seems less to get to a place with ease than for riders to circle incessantly, looking for mudholes and steep hills to test their mettle. Bare soil succumbs to erosion from logging, from roads and trails and from the constant traffic that does not allow a blade of grass time to root. There are so many roads and trails that the map of these for the watershed looks like a plate of spaghetti. The landscape bleeds sediment – the mud finds its way to Beaver Creek.

As part of the Blackfoot Confederacy's native trout recovery program, Matt Coombs, an independent fisheries biologist, and Elliot Fox, a member of the Kainai Nation, were engaged in a spring spawning survey on Beaver Creek. They arrived on Canada Day after a heavy rainstorm and could barely negotiate the road for mud. Matt described the stream as flowing chocolate brown in colour from the runoff.

Given the circumstances, they were a bit surprised to observe a pair of cutthroat trout attempting to spawn where the water was a bit clearer. The trout, no larger than 15 centimetres, were having trouble excavating a depression in the sediment-cemented gravel. All the mud from this event may have wiped out the eggs from other spawning cutthroat trout and created a year-class failure. For a species already on the edge, missing an opportunity to successfully spawn is a significant blow.

A grassy meadow adjacent to the spawning trout pair should have been an effective filter, keeping some of the mud from the stream, but soil compaction, wheel ruts and circular donuts from irresponsible recreational vehicle use minimized its filtering utility. One spot might not be an issue, but this has been replicated up and down the creek, plus every level spot is jammed with random campers.

As Elliot told me the story, his voice choked with emotion, seeing how his heritage had been so diminished. The disconnect between the recreational users and the struggling pair of cutthroat trout was so stark he had trouble conveying the frustration he felt about how those recreationists could be so oblivious to their impact. It was hard not to feel that same pain and frustration.

Our logging, agricultural, mining, drilling and recreation entitlements speak louder and more forcefully than does care and stewardship of the landscape. Just as no snowflake ever feels responsible for an avalanche, consistently we fail to see, or do not want to see, the impacts of all of our land-use decisions. The equilibrium between mud and water has become seriously unbalanced. But the few trout left have a message for us, if anyone is listening: restore the balance. If not, perhaps there will soon be no more trout left to send a message.

## "A HARD RAIN'S A-GONNA FALL"

The music of the sixties infuses my psyche as the wicked weather creates downpours that soak our watersheds and overflow. In my youth the music entertained me, in a melodic, mindless way. Now the lyrics speak to me in metaphor, parable and prophecy.

You might not think of Bob Dylan or Led Zeppelin as visionary voices to turn to for a sense of climate change, floods, of the role of land management or the futility of Band-Aid mitigation, but the lyrics are insightful.

Led Zeppelin, in their version of the old blues song of the Mississippi River flood of 1927, sang on the risk of levees breaking.

Dylan hit all the right chords in "A Hard Rain's A-Gonna Fall" – a funeral song of suffering.

Of course, these artists aren't hydrologists, climatologists, water or civil engineers, but there is an undeniable resonance in their messages to us that can be interpreted for issues of flooding. To all but a small group of deniers the climate is changing, and we are responsible. The reality is that the changes in climate are providing more variability, more unpredictability and more extremes in weather. To squeeze the changes into an essential nugget is difficult, but climatologists tell us it will mean less precipitation, but what there is of it will be delivered more quickly, sometimes violently.

The Alberta flood of 2013, the BC one of 2021, and indeed now every flood, is viewed as a natural disaster that requires intervention and relief for people affected. Images and stories of flood impacts make for heart-tugging narrative and good television footage. The responses reflect an emotional, politically motivated knee-jerk reaction. We could, we should, do better.

Historically, floods were natural and at times are a function of fast snowmelt or heavy rainfall concentrated along the foothills or in an isolated cell elsewhere. But now the epic nature of a flood is also partly owned by us – a by-product of hubris and ignorance over a larger scale.

In part this is the illusionary sense of invincibility and complacency provided by upstream dams and reservoirs coupled with concrete walls, riprap, river channel straightening and a variety of engineered structures. It is also the failure to remember the historical nature of our watersheds with recurring flood events, several of which were bigger than the event of 2013. Mostly, though, it is the severe disconnect with what we do on the land, where we chose to build our homes and businesses, and the path of water we intersect with roads and other infrastructure.

We should start by asking a perfectly logical question: "Why do we have floods?" Looking upstream and upslope might partially answer the question, in terms of land uses that impact the speed at which water reaches us. Then, as we look around, we might appreciate that the basic cause of flooding is an attempt to impose on the river's flood plain a development footprint that allows little flexibility in response to high water. Before we attempt to solve a problem, we have to acknowledge its source.

There is a time, and now is a good one, to think deeply and humbly about our human contribution to flood frequency, intensity and damage. We need to think anew about how our land-use decisions, especially but not exclusively in the headwaters, affect the timing and magnitude of water delivered downstream. This should be addressed by comprehensive watershed planning that breaks apart the silos of government and industry regarding logging, mining, roading, motorized recreation and the connection to flooding.

The solutions can't be piecemeal – a reach of riprapped riverbank here, a berm there and a dry dam somewhere. First, we need to heal the land from where the water comes, and now comes too fast, based on our extensive footprint. We can neither make it rain, predict where it will rain or stop it from raining. But we can affect what happens to the rain once it falls.

The tendency to call floods "natural disasters" takes away from our responsibility and the attitudinal, administrative and restorative changes required to deal with the next heavy rainfall, the next fast snowmelt, from becoming another epic "natural" disaster. More than likely floods these days are "unnatural" disasters.

More dikes, more hard surfaces, more trails and roads that funnel water, more miles of stream channel "trained," channellized, straightened and riprapped, more wetlands drained, more flood plain made unusable for its intended purpose, more forests cut, and fewer beavers, the natural moderator of runoff, are the cumulative, contributing factors to floods.

As the contributing factors, mostly of our devising and activity, rivers deliver more flood for less rain. This is not the bargain it seems, as the precipitation events that produce the devastating floods (at least to us and our infrastructure) are only marginally above normal. And we should expect more of these events.

Rivers aren't the enemy. They are simply responding and adjusting to the flow delivered from the watershed. Flooding isn't a river issue – it is landscape in scale. Dealing with flooding on the downstream reaches of rivers is akin to fighting gravity and equally hopeless. Try as we might, with our engineering prowess, we can't will gravity into submission.

No one yet has figured out how to compress water so you can store more of it in a smaller space, like a river channel. All we seem to be able to do, with all of our engineering solutions, is to move that water along faster, speeding it from one area to another. Somewhere down the line someone else is the recipient of our engineering hubris.

The traditional answers are dredge, drain, dike, dam and divert; cement it, channel it, control that water. It is a spiral, like the whirlpool of water escaping after a flush – temporary relief but not a solution.

We have entered a strange time when some are sold on the idea of plugging the rivers of the Eastern Slopes of the Rockies with dry dams as a solution to our flooding issues. The theory behind dry dams is that these large, empty reservoirs will sit perched upstream of us, and as the flood peak hits, the dam will absorb most of the water and slowly release it through ground level drains to diminish the impact.

Of course, they will have to be built to the same engineering standards and will cost as much as reservoirs that hold water. No one is quite sure yet how to keep the drains underneath the dam from plugging with gravel, rubble and tree trunks. If and when they do, and the dam overtops, the cure for flooding may end up being the cause. These issues pale beside a fundamental one of situating a dry dam downstream of where a downpour is expected to happen, because the structures aren't portable. This level of unattainable predictability would rival understanding the vagaries of the stock market.

All the miracles of engineering – of concrete, riprap, dredging, channellization and bypass channels used elsewhere with dubious results – cannot compensate for the loss of intact forests, watersheds and beaver dams that retain and absorb water.

Engineered works are designed to create resistance to flood waters – attempting to block them, tame them or thwart them. Landscapes with native vegetation, healthy riparian areas and unimpeded flood plains offer resilience, the natural ability to absorb flood water and energy, delay flood peaks and then rebound after floods. As the Borg of *Star Trek* remind us, "resistance is futile," and so it is with our single-focused, engineered solutions to floods.

The more reasonable, long-term answer is for us to treat watersheds and flood plains on new terms, exercising more care and attention. This will require a shift in public policy, of planning for watershed integrity instead of maximizing economic opportunity. For too long we have viewed our headwaters as a place to extract wealth but have not seen the wisdom of reinvesting in reclamation, restoration and protected areas. Water doesn't jump from mountaintops to our eastern border – it flows through a landscape replete with many land uses that influence water storage, delivery and flood amelioration.

Our flood plains have long been viewed as vacant real estate, flat and inviting. We need to reassert flood plains as the safety valves they are, insurance against floods. Rivers need more room to manoeuvre as climate change increases water flows. Maybe, instead of protecting people from rivers, we need to protect rivers from people.

We cannot, indefinitely, subsidize people to protect them from the extremes of weather. What we can do is help people understand the risks, rescue them from the folly of living on flood plains, and ensure flood-prone areas remain undeveloped.

Some see rivers as channels, canals, as ditches to efficiently convey water past us as fast as possible. We need to stand back and see rivers as a continuum from the trickles in headwaters, a living entity that connects us to our upstream neighbours as the downstream ones are connected to us.

When the rain falls, as Dylan says it will, what are the chances we will be ready to receive it with appropriate scope and scale actions capable of limiting the next "flood disaster?" Will the relentless beat of structural solutions to flooding continue after the rain? Or will we reach a point of engineering exhaustion and start to think more strategically and systemically about long-term solutions?

## LISTEN TO ITS SONG
### *The Sheep River*

———

In the beginning there was ice, and the Earth had no visible form. With snowfall the glacier grew, and gravity bore the ice mass downslope. This was not pristine ice suitable for a high-ball. Instead, it was permeated with bits of mountain the glacier had ground up. Like a great kitchen grater, the glacier gouged out the valley that in the fullness of time the Sheep River would flow through, delivering the melted remnants of that ice mass. The Sheep River is the daughter of ice and the progeny of erosion, flood and drought.

Indigenous Peoples named the river after bighorn sheep, still found in the headwaters and canyon walls. Peter Fidler, from the Hudson's Bay Company, on his 1792–93 trek referred to the Sheep River in his journals. The river has a rich history.

From the headwaters to its confluence with the Highwood River, as the crow flies, is about 107 kilometres. But the river twists back and forth, in torturous turns not unlike the response of a garden hose when the tap is cranked full on, so the distance is an underestimate.

The Sheep River has its origins in the protected landscapes of Kananaskis Country, Bluerock Wildland Provincial Park and Sheep River Provincial Park. Avalanche slopes roar with meltwaters coursing down drainages more vertical than horizontal. Headwater streams have a constant rumble as rocks are propelled downstream with the racing flow. It is as if a colossal, elemental gravel crusher is at work endlessly agitating and grinding the edges from frost-shattered rocks, making them rounder and more easily moved. This process of turning big rocks into little ones becomes especially relevant to downstream water storage in alluvial gravels, shaded by a luxuriant riparian forest.

Downstream of Gibraltar Mountain the river starts to incise, forming a steep-sided canyon often over a hundred metres deep that persists until just upstream of Turner Valley. As it carves its way downward, there are places where the backbone of the mountains will not break. This includes Sheep Falls and Triple Falls, but there are numerous other bedrock infringements on a river's rights. The river has patience on its side, sandpapering and polishing the bedrock. Resistance is futile, but the bedrock budges minimally, over the kind of time we cannot fathom.

It is here that the river is loudest, complaining of the hoops it has to jump through to deliver water downstream. A colleague who worked at the nearby Gorge Creek biological station recalled hearing the grinding and clashing of large boulders driven downstream by the turbulent spring flows.

The Sheep River canyon holds some unique memories for me. I worked one spring with colleagues to electrofish the canyon, in search of mountain whitefish thought to overwinter in deep pools. Entering the dark canyon, only minimally lit by the spring sun, seemed like a trip into the bowels of the Earth. We caught a handful of mountain whitefish, dispelling the theory that the canyon was their overwintering lair.

The native fish complement, in addition to mountain whitefish, was bull trout, westslope cutthroat trout, longnose suckers and white suckers. Early sportsmen, with European roots, lobbied for trout stocking, mostly of non-native rainbow trout, to shore up what they believed were population declines. The unique genetic adaptation of native cutthroats was overwhelmed with rainbow trout genes. The "Johnny Appleseed" mentality pervaded, and from 1928 onward until the early 1970s rainbow trout, brown trout, brook trout, and non-native cutthroat trout were stocked in the watershed.

Ironically, it was in Gorge Creek where Dr. R.B. Miller, an early fisheries researcher, investigated the madness of stocking hatchery trout in streams already home to native populations. Miller found hatchery trout, not used to the rigours of a stream environment, mostly died, often within days of stocking. Still, the idea that streams needed hatchery help took a while to die.

Bull trout populations, elsewhere doing poorly, seem to be rallying in the Sheep River. Jay Jones, an avid angler, has noted an expansion of the area where they spawn, signalling a population increase. Bow River rainbow trout migrate into the Sheep to spawn in a reach through Okotoks. But Jim Stelfox, a retired provincial fisheries biologist, points out that excessive water withdrawals create low flows and, coupled with increased water temperatures and treated sewage releases, this leads to periodic and chronic fish kills. A failing grade is given for trout kills.

What trout need to survive are stream habitats that are cold, clean, connected and contain complex elements. The presence and abundance of trout populations is a metric of watershed health and a report card on the way we manage land use in a watershed.

In a prior administrative life, the Sheep River headwaters were part of the original great sweep of forest reserves of the Eastern Slopes. Although they were set aside for watershed protection, there was logging and coal mining, but at relatively minor scales.

Selective logging with a minimal footprint was the order of the day, using axes, crosscut saws, manpower and horsepower. Contrast that with today's industrial scale operations (on tributaries like Wolf and Coal creeks) where timber is mown down like wheat in a field, leaving great expanses of the forest denuded and subject to erosion.

No environmental regulations were in place during the discovery and development of oil and gas resources from 1914 through to 1946. One can only speculate on the materials flushed into rivers, and petrochemical contamination may be an enduring legacy of the boom period.

Breezes no longer stink with the smell of unrestrained exploitation, and only ruffle the leaves of cottonwoods in the wider valley of the Sheep starting near Turner Valley. Here the river becomes braided, with multiple channels and a riparian fringe of treed summer greenery. You can hear the river murmur over gravels, the former boulders and rocks from the mountains ground down to size.

The valley of the Sheep has a deep, wide bed of gravel and the river flows on the surface, beside the channel and beneath it. No wonder the water-loving cottonwoods, willows, red osier dogwoods and saskatoons across the flood plain prosper. Coincidentally, amid the traffic noise is a cacophony of summer birdsong, for those inclined to listen.

Unsurprisingly, humans have always gravitated to the places where wood, water and shelter made survival possible. Once there, as Chris Mills, an Okotoks resident, observed, "We have chafed at the warnings and restrictions imposed by the river." In flood, the river roars with a voice not to be ignored and sweeps away the puny attempts to constrain it. In drought years, the supply of water does not equate to thirsty wishes. It would be better if we recognized limits and learned to bend with the river.

Trying to bend the river to our wants is costly, it sacrifices much of the amenity and ecological values of the valley and, in the final analysis, is futile. Big rock (Okotoks) is a fine name for a town but piled on the riverbanks – hardly! A mountain of boulder and concrete riprap now covers almost seven kilometres of riverbank from Turner Valley to the mouth. An observant colleague points out there are two types of bank armouring – the type that has failed and the type that will.

Straightening and straitjacketing the channel and covering the flood plain with roads, buildings and parking lots compounds problems of flooding. Intact flood plains absorb and store flood water, dissipate energy, reduce erosion and add to groundwater storage, invaluable for future thirsty times.

Fitting communities to the river, especially for flood protection, suggests the best way to protect people from floods is to protect flood plains from people. In every flood the river delivers the same, time-worn message – stay out of my way. The question becomes, is there anyone listening?

On this, Mike Murray, from the Bow River Basin Council, provides a valuable perspective: "Watershed stewardship groups coalesce around the thought that a community of interests can help direct a course for a shared landscape, providing vision, support and cooperation." With such engaged individuals, rivers and their watersheds develop a voice and friends.

John Scott Black, an early southern Alberta media broadcaster (and avid angler), once told me that what is ignored and overlooked is something doomed. With the announcement of the construction of a dam that would drown three rivers, the Castle, Crowsnest and Oldman, he bemoaned the fact that these rivers lacked enough friends to thwart their eventual demise. In a similar way, if the Sheep River lacks enough friends, visible champions and visionary local and provincial politicians and bureaucrats, then it will be in a dangerous position.

Canadian folk artist Connie Kaldor sings of going up the Sheep to climb a mountain, cool her feet in its flow and to breathe the Rocky Mountain air. The song is a dream, a poignant memory of the Sheep River. Dreams can be evocative bookmarks but alone do not guarantee the persistence of the reality that created them. The Sheep River as it once was, maybe still is, may slip away unless there is awareness, knowledge and the will to ensure it continues to inspire and provide its other gifts to us.

The Sheep River has a song rich with layers of meaning and expression. If you listen, have taken the time to hear, the song has a complex message. The message is eons old and as new as today. It says a river is a unified, integrated system, upstream to downstream, channel to riparian, and visible water to subsurface flow – it cannot be divided into parts and expected to function.

The river sings to us, about us. It speaks to what changes and what stays the same. What we need and what we don't. What is precious, what is lost and what is gained. How we can be washed away in ignorance, hubris and greed. Mostly, the song reminds us why we should care for a river that provides so much and requires some respect in return.

## QUESTIONS FROM A RIVER

If rivers were sentient beings with the faculty of communication, they might ask some difficult questions. Why do we give them such confusing and contradictory advice? Why are they blamed for our mismanagement? If they provide us with the essential ingredient for life and livelihoods – water – why is that value and service so unappreciated? Don't we realize that rivers go far beyond just providing for our economic possibilities? How can we be so blind to the needs of rivers?

We ask them to slow down, with dams; speed up with channelization and riprap walls; go here, not there; and stay away from where we have built but be close enough to be useful. There might be wry comments about muddying their waters, polluting it, sucking vast quantities away and disrupting the natural rhythms of annual flow, even as we rely on their life-giving flows. It's a head-scratcher.

Rivers might be incredulous that we would blame them for floods, especially the extreme, repetitive ones. Rivers might rightfully argue they don't cause floods – they merely provide the conduit for flood waters. Flood waters that are, in part, exacerbated and accentuated by logging clear-cuts, a latticework of roads and, sometimes our flood control measures. The raging flow, spilling out, consuming bridges, fields, houses and stately cottonwoods as the river gags on water that could have been absorbed for a later slow, sedate release. Blaming the river is like blaming the hammer that you used to hit your own finger.

We remove large volumes of water, often when rivers need those flows most to revitalize their beds and banks. It seems like multiple abuse: blame for flooding, then throttling back on flow later, to starve the river. In a poor bargain, we replace these essential flows with a dribble of often polluted return water.

Rivers might shake their heads at the inconsistency of wanting them to be at our beck and call, upstream and down, and always provide flows of sufficient quantity and quality when we indiscriminately divert, pollute and ignore seasonal rhythms. Rivers might ask why we don't apply the golden rule of treating our downstream neighbours as we would want our upstream neighbours to treat us.

Rivers used to define us. They were often the easy ways of moving through the landscape. Their tree-shrouded valleys were shelter from summer heat and winter storm. We quenched our thirst and ate from the cornucopia of fish, wildlife and wild fruit. Rivers might wonder why we have turned our backs on them. Aren't they still important?

There was a time we respected, maybe even loved our rivers. Now, we take rivers for granted, making them our back alleys and drains instead of our front yards. It has become too easy to ignore and abuse them.

Rivers might be concerned that something ignored too long becomes something forgotten. Once we lose a vision of what a river in its natural state looks like, we slip into believing the concrete or riprap-lined trickle of stained, discoloured water is a river as it always has been. It's then hard to have an affinity for something that you must wade through waste to get to, don't want to touch (or drink) and certainly don't want to linger around.

We can begin, again, to respect and honour our rivers. There are indicators that can tell us if a river is healthy or, if missing, can inspire us to consider some restoration. Rivers appreciate flows that have natural variability, since variation in flows is critical to the ecosystem that a river supports.

Spring floods are essential to reset the ecological clock, providing new sediment bars for the seeds of cottonwood trees to establish. Substrates of gravel are cleansed of sediment and new pools are created, mandatory for aquatic life. Our engineering works strive to even out flows and provide the illusion of flood protection, contrary to what the river needs. If asked, a river would prefer not to be a canal, or a ditch.

A river without water, or even much water, ceases to be a river, so a river would appreciate it if an adequate and appropriate amount of water always flows down its channel. There are ecological imperatives and thresholds for the right amount of water. Suitable flows maintain the structure of a river channel – its pools where fish escape the ever-present current and riffles where the agitation of the water over cobble and boulders entrains air, allowing the aquatic community to breathe. When these flows occur, the wastes we flush into the river are assimilated and cleansed, much to the relief of downstream users.

The riparian zone, the green profusion of trees, shrubs, flowering plants and grasses, needs river flows to water and allow regeneration of plant life. The result is a cacophony of birdsong, abundant other wildlife and a pleasant cool space for us to escape the summer sun. These are the places where we might hear the questions rivers pose. Riverside riparian zones are places to retreat to and recreate in, and where we can be inspired by nature. The deep, binding roots of many riparian plants resist the gnawing action of flow, creating a détente of sorts with erosion. If you want a stable riverbank, strap it to a tree with deep roots.

Often unseen and so underappreciated, except by anglers, are the fish species that are native to and have, over millennia, adapted to the nuances of the river. Their presence, abundance, diversity and distribution are key indicators of how well we have cared for a river and its watershed. Fish and other aquatic life are the ultimate arbiter and report card on river health. A grade of "F" needs to be avoided, and even a "D" or a "C" aren't good enough.

Health speaks to ecosystem pieces and ecological processes present and functioning in accord with natural variation. There is also resiliency, the ability to bounce back, to rebound from random sucker punches of the natural world – one made more chaotic by our actions. A river might point out that if it is healthy, there is a good chance we who depend on it are as well.

A river whispers at the edge of human life, touching us with its presence and its passing. It both stays and moves on, inquiring as it goes. To that inquiry we need to listen and respond. In answer to a river's questions, we should reply, "We need a much better understanding of you." In saying that, maybe we can aspire to treat the river better.

Realistically, rivers can't communicate with us, and it is, of course, inappropriate to ascribe to them human-like qualities, like the ability to ask questions. As a biologist who thinks rivers should command greater respect, I risk my professional credibility in suggesting that rivers can speak. But someone should ask these questions on behalf of rivers since they can't. It would honour the rivers that give us so much if we had the appropriate answers.

## STREAM OF MEMORY

Every stream starts somewhere, but sorting out that somewhere is sometimes a challenge. The ultimate source is the sky. From origins in clouds, water runs over a bed of shattered geology. The seed that starts the stream of my memory, its origins, is a tiny spring – a seep, a trickle of water hardly noticeable beneath ornately pink-blossomed monkey flowers. More water must be hiding, since within half a kilometre the channel broadens considerably, as does the depth and flow.

Every stream has hidden, secret sources of water to draw on. Only a portion of the flow is above ground and visible. Rain and snowmelt are intercepted by a matrix of trees, leaves, bark, moss, litter and soil. Until that matrix is saturated, only a fraction of the moisture immediately reaches the stream.

Each stream is an artery carrying water from the source, eventually joining with others to form a major carotid vessel called a river. There is music in the stream – wild, nonconformist and soothing. The sound is that of entrained air escaping. Rocks are the instrument of stream song when water tumbles over them in shallow riffles.

Springtime brings a roar of authority from the stream in runoff, maybe flood. Raucous birdsong follows, from males boasting of the best nest sites. Summer thunderstorms overpower the sound, but not the annoyance of mosquito hordes. Strong autumn winds cause the aspen leaves to shudder and swirl. In winter, everything goes quiet. If you listen with intent, you might hear the mountains complaining about being ground down by the water that flows in the stream.

If one could trace the flow of water in the channel, it would look like a rotating circular staircase, or a centrifugal corkscrew. Water tugs at one bank, eroding a bit, then deposits the material downstream on the opposite bank. Then the helix repeats. Stream banks alternately resist and acquiesce. The stream runs through and under forests and into the mouths of fish with ancient origins.

Even though the channel is initially narrow enough to step over, tiny trout give chase to a deer-hair fly. Even though the fly is bigger than their mouths, they are not dissuaded from trying to engulf it. Lower down the stream where there is more elbow room, bigger native trout have no trouble believing the fly is both edible and the right size.

Maybe because they are largely hidden from our view, the lives of stream-dwelling trout are both enigmatic and fascinating. Their environment is constantly shaken – not gently stirred – by natural events.

Within the span of a year, trout experience turbulent flood flows that must be like living in a Waring blender set on grind or liquify. Then stream flows can largely disappear into the subterranean gravels, leaving just enough water so that trout dorsal fins wave in the air as they move in search of deeper pools.

Winter brings thick ice cover that shrinks the pools where water is deep enough for trout to survive. Young trout burrow into stream bed gravels as water depths diminish. On the plus side, when air temperatures plummet below freezing, ice insulates the stream and it continues to flow.

There isn't much stability in a trout's life, in a tumultuous, unsettled habitat. With a lineage running to millions of years, the trout have performed an ascent into form, shape and function –

a subtle flux of adaptation and survival. Describing trout as tough could be a glib understatement.

Sometimes the stream banks, the riparian zone, are a tangle of willows, water birch and red osier dogwood, barely penetrable with body or fly rod. When there is a canopy of old-growth spruce, the understory is scant and thick moss cushions footsteps. It is as quiet as a cathedral, with the gentle murmur of the stream reminding you that this is a place of antiquity. It is a temporary sanctuary, even from a summer downpour. Except, long after the rain has stopped, the shower persists as water droplets coalesce on the needles, grow heavy and fall.

Along with the shading, the natural rebar of bank stability and the frequent addition of terrestrial insects to feed the trout, the riparian forest provides another essential bequest to the stream.

As trees topple into the stream, they create complexity, variety and the raw materials for productivity. Trees that fall across the channel become low-head dams. As stream gravels pile up on the upstream side of the trunks a channel is transformed from a steep slope, with fast-moving water, to a staircase of plunges and quiet pools. These pools become refuges for trout to escape strong currents.

Often a large spruce, with a large but shallow root mass, will fall and pivot, coming to rest parallel to the flow, lodged against one of the banks. There it will stay, armouring the stream bank from erosion and providing the overhead cover trout use to ambush prey floating by.

Smaller bits of wood are set upon by the shredders in the aquatic insect community, mostly in the caddisfly family. These insects are important wood processors, breaking down the raw material, ingesting some of it and making the energy embedded available to others in the biological food chain. Often the things we rarely see have a key role in the energy flow and nutrient dynamics that shape the biotic community up to trout, kingfishers, warblers and mink. The little things those little things do add up to big things.

Once I viewed the stream as simply a place to catch trout. I now understand the stream is a diverse, integrated and layered system of dynamic processes, functions and outputs. A stream is a place of complexity and reciprocal arrangements, all tuned over time to a range in natural variability. It is less an entity than a pageant of parts, seamlessly fitting together.

A stream needs its forest, as the forest benefits from the stream. Intact watersheds are the hinge upon which the survival of native trout swing. A trout is the sum of many things, but if you trace the chain backwards, it becomes clear that a stream without trees is often a stream without trout.

There are places along this stream where you could imagine yourself in untouched and intact wilderness. But then the illusion is shattered when you step across a threshold onto the tattered, scarred and industrialized sections with logging clear-cuts, wellsites, pipelines, off-highway vehicle trails and mudholes, plus the stomped and littered random campsites. There the stream lacks trees and shade, and you can see the sediment collecting on the stream bed. This does not bode well for the prospects of catching a trout, or for their survival. My sense of wellness, for the trout and the stream, is rocked.

The stream has a pulse that sometimes can be measured with the tools of science. For the observant, maybe the clairvoyant, the pulse can be felt when the ebb and flow of the stream has been compromised.

Streams, forests and native trout – these are not simple ciphers, easily decoded, enumerated and labelled. They are the sensations of systems with a pulse and a rhythm easily disrupted by wheels, chainsaws and neglect.

The stream of my memory isn't one stream, it's dozens, perhaps hundreds, that I have fished, surveyed, inspected or hiked alongside. Some are bereft of the questionable benefit of names. Each has created a unique memory, sometimes of solitude, sometimes of alarm. They have entertained me, educated me and humbled me. Many I have not visited in decades; some I return to regularly. All visit me, stirring my senses, haunting my dreams.

*Illustration by Liz Saunders*

# 3

# Loggerheads:
# The War in Our Forests

*The forest was shrinking, but the trees kept
voting for the axe, for the axe was clever and
convinced the trees that because his handle
was made of wood he was one of them.*

—Anonymous

## A LEGACY OF LOGGING
### *The Shame of Hidden Creek*

———

There is a special place called Hidden Creek in the head-waters of the Oldman River. Bull trout have migrated there to spawn for thousands of years. Native cutthroat trout, in precipitous decline elsewhere, also hang on in the stream by a fin. If ever there was a place where fish should have trumped logging, Hidden Creek was the place.

It seems there is no place in our Eastern Slopes unthreatened by logging. Hidden Creek was logged in the winter of 2012/13 in a rush, possibly to counter any objections to the contrary.

The footprint of a few months of activity persists now for the foreseeable future and puts bull trout and cutthroat trout, both Threatened species, in peril.

Today's commercial logging is brutal, mechanized, large scale and probably economically marginal. To make economic sense the usual rules about land use are consistently watered down by the Alberta Forest Service as a sop, perhaps a subsidy, to the timber industry.

The logging of Hidden Creek, a known and key spawning area for a threatened trout species, underscores a case of pervasive tunnel vision, essentially scorn for other forest values. In permitting the logging of Hidden Creek, the Forest Service ignored the relevance of the stream to the maintenance of bull trout populations in the entire Oldman watershed. Studies showed that the stream was the epicentre for about half of all bull trout reproduction in the upper Oldman River watershed.

Although some modifications were made to the logging plan, it was clear that logging, not watershed protection, was the driver for the Forest Service. There is a consistent theme behind decisions to log: "The answer is logging; what was the question?"

If there was a risk assessment made, it did not seem to affect the decision to log. It was left to industry to define whether the tributary streams were permanent or intermittent and what protection was required. How this was done in winter, under snow cover, is a mystery.

The *Timber Harvest Planning and Operating Ground Rules* are touted as best management practices, but the assertion is hollow, especially in light of deviations provided to industry. Construction of the logging road too close to Hidden Creek and crossing its tributaries was in violation of mandated buffers.

Logging was allowed during chinook conditions instead of only on frozen soils. Also ignored was Hidden Creek's Class A status under the provincial *Water Act*, which prohibited the crossing of tributary streams.

Oversight by the Forest Service, even to correct chronic failures in erosion protection, was noticeably lacking. There was no attempt made to monitor hydrologic response, water quality or stream flow. Without monitoring, no problems can be detected and hence no lessons are learned to be applied to other areas. If you don't look, you see nothing, learn nothing and nothing changes.

Bull trout did spawn in the fall of 2013 following logging and flooding, creating 41 redds. This coincided with a "windshield" inspection by the Forest Service, who concluded that logging had not affected spawning success. This seemed to be the only "official" monitoring of the effects of logging on the spawning population of bull trout in Hidden Creek. This, despite the fact that it was the responsibility of the Forest Service to monitor effects on a Crown-owned and Crown-managed forest. Following 2013 there was an 80 per cent reduction in bull trout redds. In 2019 only a single bull trout female managed to excavate a redd.

Spray Lake Sawmills, the logger, applied no special provisions to protect the stream, other than the minimum required by the Forest Service. Even these were performed in a perfunctory manner, especially the installation of sediment barriers. On one tributary stream the sediment barrier was missing, but a roll of the material was lying unused in the brush, near the stream. The timber industry speaks of a stewardship commitment, but the results speak louder than their words.

Fisheries managers suspended annual bull trout redd counts before the effects of logging and flooding could be monitored. One excuse was that these did not provide detailed enough information to assess population fluctuations. While it is true redd counts are a crude assessment of trends, they are better than doing nothing, which seems to be the current direction. Without volunteers stepping up to the plate and providing long-term annual redd counts it would have been impossible to assess the impacts of flooding and logging on spawning in Hidden Creek.

When aspects of ecological integrity, like bull trout spawning, aren't regularly and robustly measured and monitored, we can't assess population trends, understand the effects of land-use decisions or take corrective actions that protect biodiversity, especially species at risk. There is a cost to inaction – species disappear. Even an accurate compass can put you on the rocks if no one is paying attention and watching.

So who benefited from the logging of Hidden Creek? The government of Alberta made a few bucks on stumpage fees. The logging company profited from a cheap timber supply as well as a preferential interpretation of the logging rules, lackadaisical regulatory oversight and minimal reclamation standards. The last three are an indirect form of subsidy, effectively reducing the costs of logging.

How did bull trout fare in this "Alberta Advantage"? There were at least six years of lost reproductive potential, which will be difficult to recoup. Bull trout with fidelity to spawning in Hidden Creek had few other alternatives, since other watersheds with some spawning potential are significantly impacted by logging, roads and off-highway vehicle traffic.

The saga of logging Hidden Creek is a cautionary tale of failures of responsible agencies and the timber industry and, more importantly, the inability to acknowledge and learn from mistakes. These are recurring problems with logging up and down the Eastern Slopes. This will not be corrected until all the actors take responsibility for their actions and realize the forest is more than standing dimensional lumber.

The cutblocks on Hidden Creek won't be logged again for over a hundred years, based on slow, torturous growth rates in a circumstance where trees struggle. The ones cut were over a hundred years old and barely 20 centimetres in diameter at their bases. When those trees were seedlings, about 1900, far-sighted and wise bureaucrats were thinking about and instituting a landscape approach to watershed protection called the Forest Reserve. Sadly, that noble ideal has been exchanged for one of exploitation, a shift for areas originally set aside for their watershed virtues.

Maybe, just maybe, by the time the feller bunchers or their new kin come again to Hidden Creek there will be a more enlightened approach to forest and watershed management than that exhibited by recent logging. If bull trout and cutthroat trout (as well as grizzlies, elk, wolverine, and lynx) survive this latest logging onslaught, they might persist until the next one.

The best we can hope for, those of us who appreciate clean water, native trout and watersheds with ecological integrity, is the Forest Service going extinct before many of the biodiversity indicators of enlightened, sustainable forest management do.

## STUMPING THE FOREST

Usually, people of my advanced age group are favourably disposed towards fibre, both for the physical constitution and the moral one. But I find myself more and more anti-fibre when I witness the ongoing war in the woods over industrial, clear-cut logging.

Each generation has its own rendezvous with the land; it would seem today's Forest Service and the industry are at least a generation behind today's public, who want their forests managed for more than dimensional lumber. The spectre of logging in several sensitive southwestern Alberta watersheds reinforces this dichotomy.

The impression one is left with in reviewing the actions and intent of our Forest Service in these disputes is an agency out of touch, lacking a unifying sense of forest values. Observers might conclude that leaving forests to the care of the Forest Service is akin to leaving a pig under the protection of the butcher. In one case all that is left is the squeal, in the other just sawdust, stumps and sediment.

Forests are more, much more than fibre, described as dimensional lumber, fence posts and now bark mulch for landscaping. But fibre vision, a variant of tunnel vision, has become a debilitating disease in which perception and reason are restricted by arrogance and ignorance. Vision is further distorted by vested economic interests and politics.

If left untended the malady progresses to a type of institutional blindness, in which no other forest attribute or value can be discerned. Its legacy, other than rotting stumps and eroding skid trails, includes streams filled with silt, a ravaged landscape that has lost visual interest, an unnatural quiet, with no trees to capture the wind or shelter birds, and a vacant space, across which wildlife are reluctant to travel.

As for the foresters who design the logging plans, the bureaucrats and politicians who push them over citizens' concerns and the corporate directors who collect the profit from deforestation, they will soon be extinct. But we must give them their due – they are doing their very best to take with them creatures whose residence in these watersheds is at least 12,000 years longer than theirs.

That which exploiters fail to value, or do not value, they take no trouble to comprehend. To clean water, cutthroat trout, bull trout, grizzlies and connections, only lip service is paid.

The Forest Service and the industry, in their antiquated public input process, suck the oxygen out of legitimate debate over forest management with the time-tested "DAD" approach (Decide-Advise-Defend). Whatever the public process is, the deal is rigged and participants end up wasting time and energy on something our Forest Service and the industry were really never engaged in anyway.

Any goodwill engendered by asking the public to participate is squandered and rapidly evaporates into anger towards an agency still in a command-and-control mode. The rush to cut trees because they are getting older supersedes forest management for multiple values, and meaningful engagement with Albertans who care about their forests.

I know there are still professionals in our Forest Service who care about forests and have the public interest as a focus. These voices of reason, balance and restraint are overwhelmed by the politics of timber harvest.

If you plan, in the future, to drink water, enjoy a forest land-scape, fish and hunt or watch wildlife, now is the time to pay attention to the rapid industrialization of our forests. The focus should be less on wood fibre and more on moral fibre in forest management. A lack of public oversight now will doom us to a new Alberta coat of arms displaying a field of stumps where forests once stood.

## TROUT IN HOT WATER
### *Native Trout Don't Sweat, but They Do Feel the Heat*

Last summer I dipped my hand in the flow of one of my favourite trout streams. Expecting a frigid response, I was surprised by how tepid the water was, like bathwater allowed to stand.

Which stream was I on? I recall the late conservationist Bob Scammell saying in response to revealing a favourite stream, "Fish and tell and go to hell." I have no desire to go early to that hot place, but I fear we have consigned, or will, many of our trout populations to that fate. As a spoiler alert, don't expect there to be trout fishing in hell.

The mechanisms and causes of that warm water in my favourite trout stream are multi-faceted, complex and interwoven. Of course, the overarching issue is climate change, a function of greenhouse gas (GHG) emissions from the enthusiastic burning of fossil fuels. Denials about climate change notwithstanding, human activity, including Alberta's contribution, is heating up the Earth and adding to the trouts' predicament.

Dr. Stefan Kienzle, from the University of Lethbridge, has painstakingly assembled climate data from a 67-year period

(1951–2017) that shows Alberta's climate has been warming. In short, for my trout stream, and others, the trend has been for more warm and hot days, less snow, more spring rain, less summer rain and, overall, less precipitation.

It doesn't take sophisticated modelling simulations to understand warmer water temperatures will soon predominate, watersheds will become thermally unstable and headwater streams will become isolated due to thermal fragmentation.

Why would increasing the Earth's thermostat matter to trout? Trout didn't evolve to swim about in tepid bathwater. From their origins in glacial meltwater, native trout exist, survive and thrive in cold waters.

Native Alberta species like westslope cutthroat trout, bull trout, Arctic grayling and Athabasca rainbow trout have thermal water preferences between 4° and 14°C. This is the Goldilocks factor for trout, the just-right range of temperature. Temperatures above 20°C are judged to be "life-threatening" by most researchers. In some cases, if water temperatures exceed the thermal preference limit of 14° for even a few days, trout no longer occupy those stream reaches.

Since trout are "cold-blooded," water temperature governs much of a trout's life – setting in motion their entire life cycle. Shifting the temperature upwards throws a wrench into that delicate balance of life, a dance with their environment they have maintained for several millennia.

Water temperature increases are particularly vexing for westslope cutthroat trout. Not only does warmer water upset their life cycle, but it also threatens them with crossbreeding with non-native rainbow trout. Warmer stream temperatures allow rainbow trout to move upstream into the remaining cutthroat habitats and increase the chances and risks of hybridization.

How does a watershed function under climate change? First is less winter snowfall. Watersheds are water batteries – they need recharge with winter snow, which should linger, melt slowly and in large part be absorbed into shallow underground reservoirs. Warmer winters have shown us that instead of snow we get rain – rain that runs off over frozen soil, not contributing to groundwater.

Rain on a leak-proof layer of frozen ground provides about as much benefit to summer stream flow as would that from a paved parking lot. Less snow to melt means less cool meltwater through summer heat and thus less water in streams throughout the summer months. Low stream flow allows solar radiation to warm streams faster.

Hidden from view is the incredible volume of snowmelt that is held in the layers of gravels beneath the soil. This refrigerated water slowly seeps back into surface flow, cooling summer stream temperatures and, in winter, providing water warmer (by comparison) to surface flows that is key to successful over-winter survival of trout. Without this reservoir of groundwater, streams would cease to flow in winter and Eastern Slope streams would contain no trout.

The shift from snow to rain, especially more spring rain, means the intensity and magnitude of flood risk is increased, adding one more strike against trout that spawn in the spring. If that initial and key surge in runoff passes without adding measurably to groundwater storage, diminished summer flows result, which trout can't rely on. Unlike snowmelt, summer showers are the "here today, gone tomorrow" type, adding little to later stream flow. Low flows going into the fall and winter disadvantage trout that are fall spawners. Climate change and land use have a major effect on groundwater.

How does natural plumbing work and why do trout need an intact forest? Forests of the Eastern Slopes provide the source, the support and the critical element that sustain trout – water. Intact, unfragmented forests slow the movement of soil water so streams that draw from these mossy "sponges" have even, dependable flows. The forest canopy, multiple metres tall, shades stream channels, stabilizing and keeping water temperatures cool. Cold, road-free and intact watersheds are the hinge upon which the survival of native trout swing.

A new breed of forest hydrologists, not married to forestry agencies or companies, questions the old paradigms of forest management and the effects of logging on stream flows. Their research, growing in volume, concludes that logging substantially affects the hydrological processes that generate stream flow, by altering the natural flow regime. Trout are the first in line to feel this, as shifts in the stream flow regime have substantial consequences, including the timing of water delivery, energy dynamics, sediment amounts and nutrient availability.

Forests are complex and so too are the effects of logging on them, as I have learned from Dr. Kim Green, one of the new wave of forest hydrologists. The basics are that a forest canopy dampens solar radiation and reduces wind effects, both of which hasten snowmelt. Removal of the forest canopy leads to more snow accumulation, but results in faster snowmelt, greater water runoff, more floods, earlier floods and bigger floods.

These conditions can persist for decades (up to 100 years), post logging. It's not so much how much extra snow a logging cutblock accumulates – it's how much snowmelt is trapped and stored as groundwater that makes the difference. These conditions occur even with moderate to low levels of logging.

The flashiness of watersheds following logging (how quickly they respond to precipitation) is a function of several things. Logging roads and trails capture and divert water from natural drainage channels, adding to flood risk and enhancing erosion. Stream flows rise with greater solar radiation exposure, found in logged watersheds – so every time it warms up during the freshet the stream will peak.

Dr. Green points out that with increased flood frequency and magnitude comes additional stream energy that can mobilize stream bedload, increase bank erosion and alter the form of streams, including over-widening the channels. She refers to the stream channel getting "ruffled" in these events. These wider, shallower stream channels warm up faster.

We can't change how much moisture falls on the landscape, but with a large land-use footprint it is delivered to stream channels faster. Spring melt is the one shot for water capture to provide sustained flows the rest of the year. Hastening that melt, speeding it on its way, means stream flows suffer, beginning in summer and persisting through fall and winter. Summer stream temperatures rise as an added impact. Trout don't sweat but do feel the heat.

There are the little things that add up to be big ones. Streamside buffers of unharvested forest are touted as the mitigation for industrial activity in the uplands. These are generally set at 30 metres wide (on each side of a stream), despite the research that points out that for large wood debris recruitment, sediment control, sediment removal and temperature moderation, buffers up to 100 metres and larger are required.

Unfortunately, there is a consistent deferral to minimum buffer widths, which I presume is the result of persistent lobbying from industry.

Intermittent headwater tributaries and small, permanently flowing streams get no buffers, or ones insignificant in effectiveness. This ignores the reality of gravity and that impact upstream will flow downhill. The headwaters have not been given effective protection from a variety of land uses.

Stepping from the cool of what's left of a riparian forest into the August blast of heat in a cutblock provides an excellent sense of why wider buffers are required to moderate temperatures. Waiting for a cutblock to regenerate to where it duplicates the shading of the previous forest canopy takes decades. That is time trout don't have.

Provincial fisheries biologists and biologists with the Alberta Conservation Association have documented that the upper portions of many headwater rivers are still within the optimal range for trout, but downstream reaches teeter on the edge of thermal suitability. All require a much higher level of management and protection if native trout are to persist.

The reason trout are in trouble is that the land-use footprint is already large and is growing in watersheds occupied by trout. More logging, mountaintop coal strip mines and unregulated recreational use is akin to throwing gasoline on a fire.

To say we are protecting our essential watersheds, in the face of evidence to the contrary, is disingenuous, and a failure to respect history. It is also an affront to future generations. Water temperature increases and habitat deterioration are entangled with past and present decisions on land use, and the effects are additive to global climate change. We have open to us a closing window of opportunity to correct this, to restore a higher level of care to the Eastern Slopes.

One thing is for certain: if we don't try, trout in my favourite stream, and others, are toast – burnt toast.

## THE LONG, UNCERTAIN ROAD HOME FOR NATIVE TROUT

"In our careers we have never known trout to be anything but imperilled."

When I heard Jessica Reilly and Laura MacPherson's wistful, sorrowful statement it gave me pause. Over their nearly 20-year careers as provincial fisheries biologists native trout have become either Threatened or Endangered.

I thought of the perceived exuberance of trout I had experienced, although my older colleagues might have said I was seeing the dregs compared to their observations. Such is the case of shifting benchmarks and our inability to detect change. In retrospect, after studying hundreds of archival photographs, I know the trout population trend in my career was decidedly negative, and it has leaked into the careers of those younger than me.

Jess and Laura (and a small cadre of others) work on recovery initiatives, but it must be disheartening to see only a distant horizon of possibilities and not a finish line. Their work – attempting to recover viable populations of native bull trout,

Athabasca rainbow trout and westslope cutthroat trout and their habitats – is the equivalent of a lunar landing, with all the uncertainty, cost and impediments.

They are up against economic imperatives to drill, log, dig, dam and otherwise convert natural resources like forests, oil, coal and water into fungible units. Industrial-scale recreation, especially off-highway vehicle use, further fragments and degrades trout habitat. A siloed bureaucracy presides over this, too insular, internally focused and mandated to meet economic goals.

Ecologically illiterate politics and policies guide these phenomena, in part due to an indifferent, disconnected public. Potential advocates like anglers are split between supporters and those who cannot grasp that they might be part of the problem.

If the resource development regimes of the past (and ones still used today) resulted in the dilemma we are in with species at risk, wouldn't it be wise to use evidence-based solutions to guide future resource extraction? Imagine if comprehensive, ecologically based land-use plans had to precede development. If the playing field were levelled out and biologists, planners, foresters, recreationists and industry worked together, consider what the outcomes might be for landscape integrity and biodiversity.

One thing is crystal clear: instead of a small group of biologists and conservation interests shouldering all of the load for species recovery, there needs to be a recognition that this is a mandated provincial and federal responsibility that cuts across administrative and corporate boundaries.

The list of necessary recovery actions might have Hercules rejoice in his comparatively insignificant 12 labours, or Sisyphus happy with his task of rolling the rock uphill endlessly. Many watersheds, now with critically imperilled trout species, have been historically ravaged with an extensive, sometimes still-growing human footprint, and it is difficult to know where to start.

A trout's body has been modelled by the world it evolved in. Unfortunately, as we continually change that world – the flow patterns, the chemistry, the physical habitat and the temperature – the body can't keep up. Adaptation isn't based on a stopwatch, but by a march of time beyond our comprehension.

There is uncertainty about the best, most cost effective and most robust trout recovery actions given the range of species, risks, threats and current watershed states. This can only be alleviated by doing more, learning and applying that learning to new recovery tasks. Most pressing is that there is very little time left to accomplish long-term recovery work before some populations could disappear. Native trout are running out of time. Or time is running out of them.

As Jess and Laura and other biologists know in their hearts, and maybe their souls, once a wild creature with a tenure thousands of years in the making winks out, there is a void that cannot be refilled. The stream cannot be made whole again and future generations will have lost an essential link to the past.

Recovery of native trout populations need support now, at all levels, with all hands on deck, accompanied by appropriate resourcing if this ecological loss is to be avoided. Today's biologists and a legion of new anglers and watershed supporters, many yet unborn, need to have the chance to experience a world that has very nearly slipped from our grasp. If we don't act fast, it certainly will.

## HOW MUCH DID THAT 2X4 COST?
### *Logging's Unseen Toll*

———

Everything has a price – how much you need to pay for it. There are also a series of benefits, especially to those who provide that product, and, for provincially owned resources, the rents, royalties and payments made to the public coffer. In that realm are also the employment benefits and the taxes paid by workers and corporate bodies. You will have to shell out somewhere between $4 to $5 for an eight-foot 2x4. That's the usual retail price sticker. But what's the cost?

Economists, politicians and lobbyists are constantly adding up all the economic benefits of the business side of the equation. If answers on the plus side seem inflated that's because rarely are the full costs of an endeavour ever calculated.

Part of the problem economists and others have trouble grappling with is that some of the costs are hard to calculate in strict, hard currency terms. To some, the only thing relevant is the economic benefit. Everything else is extraneous.

There are some significant externalities in that 2x4, which are rarely accounted for in logging plans. The way logging is practised is based on reducing inputs and enhancing profit. A clear-cut, with the tangle of skid trails and roads, is hardly a gentle approach to other forest values. You will recognize this if you go out into the woods today.

Large logging footprints change the hydrologic response of a watershed, speeding runoff and exacerbating flooding. Intact forests store water – logged ones don't. More sediment is added to receiving streams, reducing water quality for downstream users. Fish and wildlife populations, some of which are categorized as Threatened or Endangered, are put at substantial risk. Some will wink out of existence if the present practices continue.

It's doubtful we will attract much in the way of tourists to gaze on fields of stumps, sediment and sawdust. Adding to the logging footprint will compound our climate change woes, especially in reducing the moderating effect of intact forests on floods and droughts. Logging does nothing to minimize wildfires, despite the rhetoric of the forest industry.

Despite this, successive Forestry ministers have ratcheted up the extent of logging – industrial-strength clear-cut logging – especially in the Eastern Slopes, our essential watersheds. It would seem all other forest values are extraneous to them. Unfortunately, many Albertans who hold the Eastern Slopes dear have had little success in engaging in a meaningful, timely and transparent discussion with the Forest Service or the forest sector. It is as if logging is baked into the decision, it is the answer, and any questions are irrelevant.

The stock response from the forest sector goes along the lines of "We follow all relevant rules and regulations." Even if that were true, it would be important to understand they have lobbied successfully to substantially reduce the effect of the rules on their economic bottom lines. Regulations might be effective if they weren't administered by a captured agency – the Forest Service. The amount of regulatory oversight is minimal. We shouldn't be fooled by the dubious greenwashing certification programs the industry hides behind.

Timber harvest, especially the scale of logging in the Eastern Slopes, should demand some analysis, some full cost accounting of this land use. A transparent approach of assessing not just the benefits but also all the costs would put all of us in a better position to understand if the present system is in the public interest. It would be best to do this before logging plans are set in stone and the feller bunchers are unloaded. This is especially so for our sensitive headwater watersheds in the Eastern Slopes.

Cigarette packages are now arrayed with horrific pictures and health warnings of the cost of smoking. Maybe a similar approach for timber products would jolt us into understanding the costs of today's logging practices.

Full cost accounting would tell us what we're sacrificing for that 2x4. If the sticker price included the real costs, it might persuade us to ask for genuine, sustainable logging practices, instead of today's cut-and-run ones.

*Illustration by Liz Saunders*

# 4

# Change: It's Inevitable, Except from a Vending Machine

*Never doubt that a small group of thoughtful,*
*committed citizens can change the world.*
*Indeed, it is the only thing that ever has.*

—Margaret Mead

### SEEKING PARADISE

Stories of paradise are not totally apocryphal. Having spent time reading the journals of early explorers, travellers and surveyors, I realize they all cannot be accused of telling tall tales. Early photographic images of the bounty of fish and wildlife tell a compelling story about the paradise that was Alberta.

This paradise attracted my grandparents, although it may have been the lure of free land through the auspices of the homestead era coupled with the largely inflated and rosy projections of superior farmland, shilled by the federal government.

My maternal grandparents emigrated from Finland, from a history of famine and the recognition on my grandfather's part that in spite of his being the eldest, the wait for the farm to pass to him would be lengthy. He became a miner, first at Red Canyon, Wyoming, where he narrowly dodged one of the largest mining disasters in Wyoming's history. The family moved to Belt, Montana, where draconian mine bosses made life even more perilous than dealing with the risks of underground mining.

How they heard of the possibilities of Canada, in that pre-internet era, is uncertain. They moved by horse and wagon to homestead in the Kuusamo district, west of Sylvan Lake, in 1900.

My paternal grandparents moved from a plains homestead on the east side of the Nebraska sand hills. My grandfather had taken possession of this land when it was still considered "Indian Territory" at a time when the demise of Custer and his 7th Cavalry at the Little Bighorn was still considered recent news. After years of drought and grasshopper plagues (probably Rocky Mountain locusts), my grandfather came looking for a paradise that had trees and water on it, settling in 1900 for a place southwest of Sylvan Lake, in the Centreville district. He left behind his first wife in a lonely grave.

What takes shape from fragmented family stories is the difficulty of carving out a viable farm – the sheer amount of human labour to clear and break land, plant crops and harvest them. While there may have been road allowances, what existed were trails, and these were dotted with mudholes, often impassible even with teams of horses. There was the slow acquisition of assets, of machinery, of additional land and of community building. Both my grandfathers were instrumental in establishing schools for their children, to give them a foundation for life.

My mother talked of attending one of those schools. The homestead was a little less than a kilometre, as the crow flies, from the little country school of Kuusamo. One needed to be a crow to traverse that distance easily when my mother started school in 1912. She related to me it would take her and her siblings about an hour to an hour and a half to circumvent all of the wetlands, sloughs, willow jungles and aspen forests that stood in their way. Even given the propensity of children to dawdle as an avoidance technique for school or chores and taking into account short legs, the image of the landscape in that era is hard to get one's head around.

Since she told me that story, I've had a hard time coming to grips with the sheer amount of landscape change that has occurred in an area I thought I knew. As a test a few years ago, I set off from the homestead to walk to the site of the old Kuusamo School. Even though two fencelines slowed me down, I walked that distance in about 20 minutes. The walk took me through the cultivated monotony of a field where my grandparents and their neighbours had tamed the bush, drained the wetlands and dried the country up. Such incredible changes in about one human lifespan!

I understand that my grandparents had to tweak paradise to make a living. While they might not recognize the landscape of today, it is doubtful we could fathom the one they started with at the turn of the last century. They would have missed the passage of the last of the buffalo across the aspen parkland by about two decades. The last grizzly was killed, just south of their homesteads, in 1894. The country was made safe for the cow and the plow, and now we are faced with the task of making the country safe from the cow and the plow (and other developments).

My comparatively easy life was made possible through the changes they made to paradise. In the foreword to *A Sand County Almanac*, Aldo Leopold wrote: "Like winds and sunsets, wild things were taken for granted until progress began to do away with them...These wild things, I admit, had little human value until mechanization assured us of a good breakfast." The cost of a pacified paradise is that now we have the "luxury" to consider protecting the pieces of it that are left.

The vision of paradise has shifted, now that we are assured of breakfast. At the site of the old Kuusamo School I noticed it was now a wildlife reserve, the land donated by my Grade 1 teacher. It's a tiny piece of real estate, but it had the look of what the country might have resembled 120 years ago, so it's a ray of hope.

Back at the homestead, my cousin showed me the trees they have been planting, to restore a little wildlife diversity and for the beauty an aspen forest can display. I think of my grandparents, who cut down the aspen and willow forest with axes, wrestled the roots out with stump pullers and grub hoes, and turned over the soil with horse-powered breaking plows.

I wonder if my grandparents were spinning in their graves over this tree planting madness. It would seem every generation sees the wisdom of their own actions, but only in the light of their own times. The wildlife reserve and the tree planting are acts of stewardship, largely altruistic actions to counterbalance a diminishing paradise. My grandparents and other pioneers killed much of the paradise they settled on, but will another vision of paradise emerge?

Pieces of paradise may survive or be restored with actions like those of my old teacher and my cousin's tree planting. I've seen many Earth Days come and go since the early 1970s. They brought environmental awareness, but environmental literacy still needs to be grown before the results are evident. Despite our being awash, often up to our hips and higher, in a flood of plans, policies, codes of practice, strategies, bylaws and legislation, paradise continues to be eroded.

I've been in the conservation business for a little over five decades. In that time, I've participated in and measured the restoration of some of the damaged bits, albeit on a shoestring of expenditure with postage stamp outcomes. I've watched the landscape change and be transformed and have observed some of the losses from the direct and collateral damage of our economic choices and decisions.

It shows we lack a collective view of paradise, maybe always will. If the view of it reflects a frontier to be exploited, then what is left will disappear as surely as the Cheshire cat in *Alice in Wonderland*. If it all trickles through our fingers, where will subsequent generations find their paradise?

## ENLIGHTENMENT
### *The Dying Age?*

I had awoken with a sense of unease. It was dark, very dark, and still. I lay, cocooned in a sleeping bag on a thin Therm-a-Rest, in a backpacking tent, listening intently to what sounded like the soft padding of footsteps outside. Sleeping in a tent, so near to the ground with just a couple of layers of rip-stop nylon between you and the outside world, exposes and intensifies your vulnerabilities.

My wife and I and our dog, a yellow lab, were in a camp-ground in Jasper National Park. Entering the park, you are warned – with huge signage about wildlife, especially bears – how dangerous some wildlife are, their unpredictability and why you must keep your distance.

At the entrance to the campground and liberally sprinkled through the campground were signs inviting one to understand you were in bear country. At check-in we were again verbally warned of bear presence and about proper food storage. To em-phasize the point the warning was accompanied with written materials. On the surface of the picnic table was a plastic notice warning about proper food storage and the dire consequences of not adhering to the advice.

Consciously and rationally, I grasped all this and the minis-cule risk we were exposing ourselves to – but my subconscious had apparently taken another track.

In our modern lives we are bombarded by advertisements, created often by the most talented of marketing professionals. We are so inundated we don't pay attention mostly, until inex-orably we are standing in a store buying "Friendship" shampoo, for which there is no logical reason for selecting that brand. Score one for the marketers.

To say my subconscious was obsessed with bears is a mild understatement. It had alerted my conscious, otherwise ra-tional mind to the sounds outside the tent. I listened with in-tent, straining to discern what was outside. I decided it wasn't human footsteps, not the mincing, prancing steps of a deer, or the heavier hoof-fall of an elk. Only a paw, a clawed paw, the paws of a heavy animal, a black bear, or worse, a grizzly, would make the soft, muffled sound moving over the spruce needles blanketing the ground outside the tent.

I lifted my head to better listen. The sound stopped, as if the animal was alert to my wakefulness. When I let my head fall, the sound continued and it seemed as I turned my head the padding would move around the exterior of the tent, sometimes fading momentarily, then becoming louder. As I lifted my head the sound would stop, reigniting the fear that the animal was aware of me. I repeated the test of lifting and allowing my head to fall back on the pillow multiple times, all with the same results. I'm sure this went on for some minutes.

I began to prepare for the worst – what if an attack occurred? The truck was locked, with our bear spray unavailable. My only weapon was my Leatherman multi-tool knife, a poor choice for warding off an attack. Could I beat the animal off with a hiking boot? Would shouts and screams bring assistance from other campers? How was I to defend my wife, which occurred to me later?

I was then aware that our dog, an animal with a highly tuned sense of hearing and smell, was sleeping soundly, blissfully, with no heightened alertness to the threat apparently just inches from the wall of the tent. This puzzled me.

Repeated tests indicated that the sound, of clawed paws, was not coming from outside the tent, nor was it clawed paws. It was the sound of my wool toque, worn to keep me warm on a frosty night, rubbing with every breath against the fabric of the sleeping bag.

I'd been had by my subconscious, reacting irrationally to the messaging of Parks Canada. What a return we get on an investment of fear, irrational behaviour and failure to use observations to moderate our reactions!

I fell back into a deep sleep after scolding my subconscious with the thought that something imagined produces more fear than the real thing. It was also a reminder to my conscious to never judge reality with a limited set of experiences and information.

This brings me to the Enlightenment, based on my enlightenment. The Age of Enlightenment, or Age of Reason, was an 18th-century intellectual movement in Europe. It came to dominate the world with, notably, an emphasis on science, reason rather than faith, based on experimentation and objective observations. This period is synonymous with the study of science, advances in scientific investigations and theories giving us the current enlightened world. Among other things, it gave us modern medicine, the internal combustion engine, flight, computers and longer lives lived with ease.

Reliance on fears, irrational explanations and faith gave way to deductive reasoning, multiple observations, and objective, evidence-based analysis divorced from preconceived notions and outcomes. This only came to me in the tent waiting for the non-existent grizzly to attack after following several lines of evidence and coming to another, rational conclusion.

Over three centuries of scientific discovery, of systematic methodology and of rational thought based on evidence seem at risk, especially with our current social media fascination with selective interpretation, unfounded rumours, hyperbolic grandstanding, conspiracy theories, outright distortions and overall uncivil behaviour. Unhelpful as well is the current 15-minute news cycle that creates a strange and perverse kind of public amnesia.

There have always been skeptics, deniers and those blindly following fads, faith and fabrication. Whether it is those who rail against immunization, believe the Earth is only 6,000 years old (and/or flat) or those who follow Elvis sightings, all have benefited from social media in their search to find their own tribe of true believers.

A milieu of sound bites, slogans and buzz words results in thought reduction, not enhancement, with few ideas but much information of dubious value. There is little rational, reasoned discussion or debate, just shouting at one another in progressively louder voices using capital letters. Tweets have turned our brains into bumper-sticker processors. In many ways it is a return to the Dark Ages of crowd mentality, false prophets and anti-intellectual leanings.

As examples, consider the following: Climate change is, alternately, a conspiracy of the Chinese to disrupt Western economies; a natural, cyclic, recurring phenomenon; or a gross misinterpretation of the data by 97 per cent of climate scientists. It is not, according to its deniers, the result of the burning of too much fossil fuel. Anyone saying differently is ill-informed, uses "junk" science and is biased against the fossil fuel industry. In response one wag wrote: "Financially strapped environmental interests have paid off 97 per cent of the world's climatologists or, multi-billion-dollar oil companies have paid off 3 per cent of the world's climatologists."

The politics of climate change is successfully waged to frustrate the "other" side, cast doubt and delay the inevitable, rather than seeking to protect your grandchildren from the very real impacts. Steve Smith, the Canadian comedian whose alter ego is Red Green, would term these people, the deniers, as "wrong, but never in doubt."

There is the corrosive effect of social media on science to create an alternative reality where facts are, if not irrelevant, at least optional. It is the place of substitution of unfounded opinion for evidence. There is faith in that for which there is no factual support – disbelief and denial about occurrences and events for which there is. The numbing thing about the tribalism inherent in social media is that your group routinely provides the conditions that spare you the need to think, and so you get out of the habit.

Brooks Atkinson, an American theatre critic and commentator, said, "People everywhere enjoy believing things that are not true. It spares them the ordeal of thinking for themselves and taking responsibility for what they know."

Science seems ever under attack by those who do not like the message, feel it impairs their freedom, limits their business and doesn't match their ideology. History provides us a rich treasure trove of examples of groups, corporations, business and, sadly, politicians who have predictably damned the messenger. We just went through this with a previous federal government where Stephen Harper silenced scientists. It happened when "communications" staff, with credentials in "spin," were tasked with message delivery, not people with backgrounds and credentials in science.

When experience, education, credibility and knowledge are debased, a world is created where Robert F. Kennedy Jr. becomes a go-to expert on immunization, Jane Fonda is an energy analyst and Kevin O'Leary the guru on fiscal policy. This signals the death of expertise and the rise of what one observer calls the "confidence of the dumb." It feeds a paranoia about science and distrust of those who provide us the results of scientific inquiry.

Science means accountability, but unfounded opinion is a pathology, one of a delusional aspect. Experts are the new pariahs – an odd place and era where people are actively scorned, not for their ignorance but for their specialized knowledge. Instead, ignorance is applauded, for in the minds of some, only the ignorant and ill-informed can truly be objective.

There is nothing wrong with ignorance as long as it is accompanied by curiosity, to seek information and knowledge. Then, a little ignorance can go a long way. But, as Elbert Hubbard, an American writer, observed, "The recipe for perpetual ignorance is: Be satisfied with your opinions and content with your knowledge."

Curiosity didn't kill the cat, stupidity did. The chaos of ignorance gives us a sense of freshness while the order of knowledge provides the frustrating curse of restricted vision.

Science is a process that is self-correcting (unlike dogma and faith). Timothy Leary pointed out, "Man's best friend is his dogma." Errors do occur in science, but the process of objectively examining new data and assessing how they correspond to current hypotheses and theories provides repeated opportunities to re-examine and revamp our understanding of how something works.

We are entering a dangerous new era, according to Charlie Brooker, an English satirist – the Unlightenment – in which centuries of rational thought and reason are being overturned by superstition, conspiracy theory, tribalism and *argumentum ad hominem*. This is aided and abetted by social media.

Wallace Stegner wisely pointed out, "Verifiable knowledge makes its way slowly and only under cultivation, but fable has burrs and feet and claws and wings and an indestructible sheath like a weed-seed, and can be carried almost anywhere and take rest without the benefit of soil or water."

Whether it is the thump in the night, climate change or other issues, the default, despite the Age of Enlightenment, seems to be to opinion, emotion, fear or disbelief instead of a rational, measured thought process based on evidence. We are, despite all our progress, not far off of the old Scottish prayer that still comforts us:

> From ghoulies and ghosties,
> And long-legged beasties,
> And all things that go boomp in the night,
> Good Lord, deliver us.

Although the hysteria, suspension of belief, and tribal thought (even when your tribe is wrong) seem to be the gifts that keep on giving despite evidence to the contrary, there are rays of hope. Some 400 years after Galileo was arrested for heresy after espousing a sun-centred solar system, Pope John Paul II apologized, acknowledging Galileo was right. Pope Francis humbly declared that scientific observations about evolution, climate change and the Big Bang are correct and God "is not a magician with a magic wand."

It's time to make a choice between wilful or blind ignorance and measured reason based on sound observation. A sound-bite culture can't discuss science very well, if at all. Scientific illiteracy leaves many unprepared and unable to discuss or understand the damage exerted on the atmosphere, habitat for wildlife or on our individual health.

We can't lower the bar on enlightenment. Tweet that!

## RESTRUCTURING EDEN
### *Shifting Our Benchmarks*

———

A friend, now retired from National Parks, has had more back-country travel experience than most of us could dream of – some of which we might have nightmares over. To fuel those travels took food, so when the going got tough, the tough found solace in food. As in life, these trips harboured no free lunches, only heavy ones. Preparation was both physical and psychological, so the food choices for a given day were based on his principle "Eat your best food first."

If you follow this line of reasoning it means the next choice, for a subsequent meal, is based on the same criterion. Of what remains, what you eat next is the best food left. Carrying this forward, at the end, when the food pack contains only oatmeal dust and microscopic beef jerky fragments – it is still your best food. This strategy has the continuing effect of buoying one up with the thought of the best left, but not about how little there is left to eat.

"Eat your best food first" could be a metaphor for the concept of shifting benchmarks. We believe we're seeing the world just fine until it's called to our attention we're not. Declines in quality and quantity persist until some tipping point of recognition is reached. Before that cliff is reached, we all think we have at our disposal a full pie worth of resources.

But in recent times we've never had the luxury of starting with a full pie, a clean slate. We think, in our blindness and ignorance, that the landscape and resources of today represent a "full pie." The reality is that today's pie is a mere slice of yesterday's pie. Today's Eden is an illusion. Nostalgia isn't what it used to be.

This shift in benchmarks, the loss of spaces and species, sometimes occurs beyond our awareness and reckoning. And so it goes – without an appreciation of the progressive thinning of the remaining slice, a healthy landscape can, and will, eventually wink out of existence, taking with it wildlife and essential ecological services.

Many of our landscapes have been disturbed and subject to change for so long it appears to the uninitiated as if this is the norm. Our benchmarks of landscape health have shifted to the level of disturbance, without realizing the impacts on aesthetics and ecosystem services, attributes and benefits. Our image shifts to the lower common denominator because we lack a reference point.

We don't have an accurate image of what the land was like before our arrival. Even by the time early explorers began to chronicle landscape features, changes were underway, with the introduction of disease, horses, improved weaponry and trade.

My grandparents homesteaded, at the turning of the 20th century, west of Red Deer, named for once-abundant herds of elk. Family stories are, however, bereft of references to elk or, for that matter, of grizzly bears and wolves, both of which were part of the landscape up to settlement. The memory of flocks of sharp-tailed grouse, and likely greater prairie chicken (now extirpated) is found in one blurred black-and-white archival image in the collective family album.

If not for the journals of Anthony Henday, Peter Fidler and David Thompson, my sense of the ecological landscape, growing up some 60 years after settlement, would be that English sparrows, rock doves and the occasional white-tailed deer were always here. Instead, they are the new normal.

Shifting benchmarks cause us (unconsciously or otherwise) to continually redefine what a natural baseline was and, in so doing, carve up the remaining but diminished pie even more.

As David Eagleman, a neuroscientist, relates: "Not only is our perception of the world a construction that does not accurately represent the outside, but additionally we have the false impression of a full, rich picture when in fact we see only what we need to know, and no more." It's the resource that shifts, but not our perception of the resource. Perception does not mirror reality. In my mind I have a 30-inch waist; my body begs to differ.

Yet we do create our own benchmarks that are accurate and useful. Many homes have a door jamb with incremental pencil marks for children's height carefully preserved. Those marks, of a child growing up, are a tangible memory of changes over time. These form family reference points. They can be so emotive that people often take the door jamb of marks with them when they move, to preserve that memory.

Sadly, those pencil marks are largely absent from the door jambs of the landscape. Most measurements of landscape health, of fish and wildlife populations, are a few decades old, and most of our history (as European settlers) is just over a century. Anything that happened before, any metric of the landscape before us, is *terra incognita*.

A benchmark is a place in time and space where we have made a point of noticing and noting as many parameters as exactly as possible so we can say in the future, that is how things were then. It is a pencil mark of landscape health, biodiversity and productivity and a mark against which we measure change.

I was stunned by the observation of an elderly angler I once interviewed. He said, "I would consider your best day of fishing today as one of my worst from my memory of past experiences." He recalled creel limits of dozens of fish, big fish, while my experience was of reduced limits and only the occasional fish on the line. His long memory, tempered with reflection, enabled him to clearly see the changes and be objective about the present.

He saw all that was missing – I saw what was there. It reminded me that by comparison, my memory was limited in scope. Benchmarks shift, like memories, from one generation to the next.

J.G. Nelson reflected in *The Last Refuge*, a history of the Cypress Hills and surrounding area, that "our memory of what we have done to the land is short and incomplete. Yet, without such knowledge, we cannot really understand how much we have changed the world and how much more we are likely to change it if present trends continue."

The process of forgetting begins with limitless things reduced first to memory, then to obscurity, and finally to fable. Some records exist in old sketches and paintings, grainy photographs and the accounts of early explorers and fur traders, reports of NWMP officers and the writings of a few historians. Very little is stored digitally, the preferred source of information in today's world, and no YouTube videos of any of this past array exist. If this had a name, it would be the "Great Forgetting."

An appreciation for history, of shifting benchmarks, could help us in planning the future of this landscape. If we have the capability to develop, to build, we also have the choice to restore, to set back the clock. It is a matter of will, not ability. If the past trajectory of losses and impairment don't cause us to reconsider present land-use levels, how will current planning position us (and our descendants) for the future?

The phenomenon of shifting benchmarks may provide lives shielded from recrimination or regret. But George Santayana warned us about failing to learn from history with "Those who cannot remember the past are condemned to repeat it." In short, this is what shifting benchmarks describe, a series of repetitive failures.

For the sake of the landscape, its vital features and ourselves, we need to develop the ability to recall the past and use it to forge a better pathway forward. That might allow us to appreciate and protect our Eden.

## COMMON SENSE
### *Really?*

What is "common sense," and is it really common? If I had a dollar for every time I have heard the expression used, especially to dismiss solutions to a complex issue and offer a simple, but wrong response, I'd be rich.

Years ago, I helped a friend move a log cabin. It was elevated on blocks and all we had to do was back a flatbed trailer under it, lower the cabin, and move it. It wasn't that simple in practice. The trailer was too high to get under the cabin without raising the structure higher. We tried that and the cabin teetered, swayed and threatened to topple off its supports. If the cabin couldn't go higher, I reasoned the trailer would have to get lower. So we took the wheels off and dragged the now lowered trailer under the cabin, jacked it up and replaced the wheels, and the move was underway.

An elderly friend with years of practical experience complimented me on my "common sense" solution. In retrospect, it was less common sense than a simple analysis of the alternatives, of which there was only one that was viable. If only all problems had that short list of alternative and clear solutions.

Common sense may be an admirable attribute in some, generally simple, circumstances, like the cabin move. There are other examples. On a snack package of airline peanuts was the product warning: "Allergy advice: May contain nuts." Probably marginally useful for children (and some adults) who require adult supervision. Guidelines on opening a bottle of wine: "Open at small end." That explains the lack of a cork at the base of a wine bottle. Or operating instructions on a clothes hanger: "Do not swallow." Anyone you see with a wire hanger protruding from their mouth clearly lacks common sense and needed the warning read to them.

There are clear limits on the application of common sense. One of the lessons of life is that for every complex problem there is a simple solution that will not work. Merely tacking the term *common sense* onto some other phrase does not confer any enhanced value to the action. "Common sense" conservation provides no better cachet to the term than would "do it yourself" nuclear fission or "self-help" heart surgery.

Many who wish to deride science and scientists make the clarion call for the application of common sense. It is a backhanded way of attacking a perceived eggheaded, book-trained "elite." For sense to be held in common must mean there are widely held beliefs about notable topics.

Descartes, the 17th-century French philosopher, mused, "Of all things, good sense is the most fairly distributed: everyone thinks he so well supplied with it that even those who are hardest to satisfy in every other respect never desire more of it than they already have." What René said is that we have an over-inflated sense of our innate ability to puzzle things out.

Common sense is defined in Wikipedia as "sound practical judgement concerning everyday matters, or a basic ability to perceive, understand, and judge in a manner that is shared (i.e., 'common to') nearly all people." The keys to the utility of common sense are the words "everyday matters" and "basic ability." The definition also depends on whom you're asking.

Often, the things that guide us in life, like physics, chemistry, biology and mathematics, lie well outside our everyday experience, leaving us little to which we can apply common sense. Common sense may have equipped us with the understanding that if we hit ourselves with a hammer, it hurts. However, it doesn't help us see that the solid, hard metal of a hammer is composed of thousands of atoms.

Every morning the sun rises. Each evening, it sets. Common sense told our ancestors the sun travelled around the Earth. All one had to do was observe a child's spinning top, a model with Earth at the centre, to discern it couldn't be in orbit around the sun.

Copernicus, the Renaissance-era astronomer, formulated a model of the universe using reason, not common sense, that Earth orbits around the sun. This was a huge intellectual leap to make, since it requires our world to hurtle through space at a speed both incomprehensible and yet imperceptible. Gravity, the invisible force, keeps us from flying off the globe. All the while we experience no sensation of great speed.

Common sense did not serve most of our ancestors well to puzzle these phenomena out. Several decades after Copernicus, Galileo was convicted of heresy by the Catholic Church for supporting Copernican theory. Common sense blinded church authorities to evidence-based explanations.

It might be a path to understanding the term if we were to associate it with conventional wisdom, something generally accepted or believed. The more one is exposed to conventional wisdom the more likely one is to become the boss of it. And, as Melissa Schilling, a professor of management, reflects: "Rigid adherence to convention and agreeableness is the sweet way to prevent independent thinking and innovation."

There are often gaps between what feels true and what scientific research says is true. Commonly held beliefs, even among some government and industry foresters, include the dual myths that logging is an ecological replacement for fire and logging prevents wildfire.

Independent forest ecologists recognize the significant difference between a tree killed with a feller buncher in a logging operation and one torched in a forest fire. Removing trees by logging creates different effects on soils, watersheds, fish and wildlife habitat, and aesthetics than if they had been killed by fire and left on site to be recycled, reduce erosion and aid in biodiversity maintenance. Logging involves an extensive road network, a significant sediment source for years.

It seems to be viewed as common sense that if a forest is logged, fire risk is removed or reduced. That might hold true if forests were never allowed to regenerate and create new fuel loads to burn. Under conditions of natural and human-induced fire starts, exacerbated by drought and wind, even young, recently regenerating clear-cuts will burn and burn intensively.

On closer examination the facts get in the way of common-sense explanations.

Models allow us to assemble the disconnected bits of information together to understand the workings of a complex system. In these situations, the dictates of common sense are not the most dependable guide to predicting an outcome. Common sense favours familiar and simple explanations over unfamiliar, complex and perhaps unpopular ones. Common sense seems so simple as to be self-evident.

A common-sense approach may not allow us to analyze data, the facts, as objectively as possible. Stephen Jay Gould wrote: "Common sense is a very poor guide to scientific insight for it represents cultural prejudice more often than it reflects the native honesty of a small boy before the naked emperor."

Realistically, what is common sense is that no one likes to see their "theories" disproven. Use of the scientific method provides impartiality, tempering human biases and blinkered vision. Science is the umpire of facts, not of defending positions.

If we were to think in ways more open and rigorous, especially on matters outside of our everyday lives, we would stand a better chance of drawing the most accurate conclusions, leading to better decisions on the issues we face every day, whether they are mundane or impactful. That is the test we should apply to common sense.

We might find common sense isn't really common, or sense. Perhaps when it is truly displayed, and useful, we should call it "uncommon" sense. Churchill said that common sense is so seldom encountered, when it is it seems like brilliance. An anonymous author said of it: "Common sense is not a gift. It's a punishment, because you have to deal with those who do not have it." The last word on common sense might go to Albert Einstein, who reckoned it was "the collection of prejudices acquired by age eighteen."

Maybe we should acknowledge that this thing called common sense might be severely overrated, beyond simple explanations and solutions. That would be common sense.

## LANDSCAPES AND BROKEN WINDOWS

The house had stood longer than most people could remember. Solid it was, built with care, attention to detail and pleasing to the eye. Saskatoon bushes rubbed up against one wall, and the intensity of the wind was muted with a buffer of spruce and aspens. Grouse sheltered under the spruce canopy, swallows nested under the eves and a robin took possession of an alcove over one of the doors. Moose occasionally browsed the saskatoons.

Inside the house was shelter – by design it was comfortable and efficient. You could tell from the fit and finish how the place was integrated, complex but coordinated, every piece having purpose and adding to the overall design.

Visibility from a new wellsite road attracted people to the place, some with less than honourable intentions. The first indignity was a broken window, then two, and finally all of them. With gaping holes, where once windows had signalled occupancy and care, a trend started. Doors were wrenched open, slamming in the breeze.

Dust and debris, along with empty beer cans and garbage from trespassing partiers, accumulated. Campfires led to random chainsaw cutting of many of the woodlot trees for firewood. Saskatoon branches were stripped for roasting wieners. Someone saw valuable board feet in the old spruce trees and off they went to become dimensional lumber instead of remaining as shelter and wildlife habitat.

Without an intact windbreak, winds swept through with a fury that ripped off shingles. Rain and snowmelt leaked into the interior, adding to rot and mould.

Instead of native grasses and wildflowers, weeds began to take over in the ruts created by motorized mischief. In a testosterone-induced, perhaps alcohol-fuelled incident, someone tried to drive their truck through the front door. With the porch damaged and rain rotting the structural pieces, parts of the house started to sag.

People began to burn parts of the house for campfires. One got out of control and scorched one exterior wall, further weakening the structure. Pigeons began to roost inside, covering the interior with their droppings.

Finally the authorities, tired of the vandalism, parties and wildfire risk, knocked the place down and burned the remainder. What was left of the woodlot was cleared and added to a canola field.

Occasionally someone would drive by, wondering what had happened to that great old house. No one remembered the birdsong, shade and saskatoon fruit. The disappearance of the place and all its virtues started with that first broken window.

The trajectory the place went through exemplifies what is called, in criminology, "broken windows theory." Visible signs of crime, vandalism and anti-social behaviour create a situation that encourages more bad behaviours. There is agreement on the part of social psychologists and police officers that if a window in a building is broken and is left unrepaired, all the rest of the windows will soon be broken. One unrepaired broken window is a signal that no one cares, and so breaking more windows has little risk. Window breaking turns to other destructive forms of vandalism.

Metaphorically, the "house" could include our natural landscapes and watersheds. How we lose the integrity, the resilience and the beauty of these places is that someone breaks one of the landscape windows, it isn't repaired, and the downward spiral begins.

Breaking windows can take many forms. It can start with a random campsite beside a trout stream – a small tent spot, a single fire ring and a bit of firewood gleaned from some deadfall. Then the trail to the site is "improved" so that trailers and bigger recreational vehicles can access the site. A small beachhead becomes a destination for off-highway vehicle users, many of them at any given time. Muddy trails then spiral out, spiderweb-like, over the watershed, more trees fall before recreational chainsaws, litter builds up and the stream is clouded with sediment after every rainstorm. People then think this is the way it has always been. No one sees the broken windows.

There can be authorized window breaking where land uses, individually approved, accumulate out of control since there is no guidance from a landscape plan, no ecological thresholds set, and no active and engaged reclamation or restoration of the human footprint. It can start with one resource road built to access one wellsite or a logging clear-cut. As with the house, once that first window is broken, the deterioration begins.

The army of ecological breakdown starts with that one road. Within a short time, often a decade or less, more roads, seismic trails, wellsites, pipelines, power lines, gravel pits, coal strip mines and others have broken all the windows in that landscape. Soon no one remembers what it was like before that first resource road. The human land-use footprint then expands into yet another watershed, with no sense of cumulative effects, limits or other landscape values.

Seemingly random acts that started small, almost innocuously, add up to a series of developments that no one initially anticipated or recognized, or that registered as a concern. We take for granted that we can have it all – the full suite of virtues and values of intact landscapes, and a full cart of developments. Somewhere along the line we forget about the former as we are overwhelmed by the latter.

Can we avoid the propensity to break landscape windows, starting a tsunami of change that seems inexorable? If we could get over the fun aspect of breaking windows and the profitability in breaking them all, there might be a chance.

It will require us to recognize the first broken windows in our landscape house, care enough to make sure they are fixed quickly, and respond better with timely, evidence-based land-use plans, to avoid the cumulative effects of breaking all the windows.

*Illustration by Liz Saunders*

# 5
# Report Cards

*Our lives begin to end the day we become
silent on things that matter.*

—Martin Luther King Jr.

## AN ALBERTA FAIRY TALE

Once upon a time there was a paradise – let's call it Alberta. It was a fine place, filled with possibilities. Fortunately for me, my grandparents, both sets, chose it to make a home. They were of proper pioneer stock, used to adversity, risk and sacrifice. I never knew them, but if children reflect their parents, my grandparents were of strong conservative stock – the conservation kind, not the political version.

It isn't as if they didn't make their mark on paradise. Farming dramatically changes the landscape. Along with the flood of others looking for paradise, they transformed a corner of it. Maybe by accident, maybe intentionally, they left a bit of aspen forest, the berry bushes and a few wetlands untouched. Their version of conservation was one of restraint. Once the basics of life and relative comforts were secured, there wasn't the acquisitive urge for more.

I doubt they would recognize the landscape of today, a blank perfection of cultivated fields. The view is interrupted by oil and gas wells, urban sprawl, drained wetlands, dry stream courses, algae-choked lakes and dust from incessant traffic. What they might see, and be appalled by, is the excess and callousness with which their paradise has been treated.

It's akin to the recklessness of hurtling down a dark and icy country road at twice the speed of sense. With bald tires, poor brakes and dodgy steering, it's hard to keep the car on the road. All there is to light up the night is one dim and unfocused headlight beam, but that's somewhat irrelevant since no one is watching the road anyway. The singularly important thing seems to be to keep the pressure on the gas pedal. Passengers are laughing, joking and having a grand time. The clink of some brown, long-neck bottles is evident on the washboard road.

If there is a niggling thought in the back of their minds, the germ of a conscience and the prescience of even fools about where, in that dark night, is the "T" intersection, it isn't immediately evident. Maybe a few are wondering, is there a sign for the intersection, will the sign be seen in time, will the dim headlight beam provide enough of a warning, and will the reaction time be quick enough to stop before there's a wreck?

That is what Alberta represents today, metaphorically. It's a mad rush to exploit all our treasure of paradise – now. As the race proceeds towards the "T" intersection, the brick wall of landscape fragmentation, increased competition for land and resources, and loss of ecological integrity, there is a hope the

"T" will magically transform itself into a four-lane, divided highway. Surely it will and we can continue to speed on, laughing and enjoying ourselves.

In reality, in the distance is a blinking amber light, maybe sometimes red, signalling a rapidly approaching reckoning. The gas gauge is hovering near empty, but not all of the inherent possibilities have been used up. A lot of things have been run over with that almost-out-of-control car. Though tarnished and a bit dishevelled, paradise still has some of the gifts of space, breathable air, mostly potable water, somewhat fertile soil and many of the native creatures. We've taken huge bites out of the present, to the point where the future is in jeopardy.

If we don't start now to slow down, read the signs and change our practices, this could end badly. The next generation will have to be extremely wealthy to pay down the debt of excess. Since many of the inherent possibilities have been used up, where will the wealth come from?

The little toehold of change created by my grandparents has become an impact crater, overwhelming paradise. Where once the wild surrounded them, now we surround it. While no one is blameless in this, it is one thing to make a living and quite another to trade paradise for a financial killing.

Instead of stock portfolios, shiny baubles and mindless consumer gifts, we can give our children more enduring gifts, notably the ability to use information to make wise decisions and a quality environment in which there are still choices left to be made. There's still time to do this, if we act quickly, to secure choices for tomorrow instead of gambling on chance. Since this is a fairy tale, the ending is what we can all make it.

## COAL IN THEIR VEINS

My uncle was an underground miner who worked for decades in Crowsnest Pass coal mines. He was a tough, stocky man, accustomed to hard work and a hard life. As he was dying in the Pincher Creek hospital a nurse tried to wash his hands, blackened by a lifetime of exposure to coal dust. He endured the scrubbing for a while and finally bluntly told the nurse, "The coal's not on me, it's in me." Indeed, coal dust was embedded in his skin and the nurse was unlikely to get his hands white again.

One might speculate what my uncle's lungs resembled, if his hands were so impregnated with coal dust. His other health issues were not as evident but were linked to his career as a miner. At a personal and a human level this is a legacy of coal mining.

Mining, for my uncle, might have been genetic. My grandfather emigrated from Finland, fleeing famine and lack of opportunity, to coal mines in Wyoming and east of Great Falls, Montana. I never knew my grandfather, but I'll bet he would have said Canada's *Dominion Lands Act* saved him from a life of mining and maybe a premature death.

My grandfather moved to what would become Alberta in 1900 and bet the government $10 against a quarter section of land he could stick it out for three years and claim the land as his. He eventually acquired other land and became prosperous, but not enough so all his sons could be set up with their own farms.

My uncle moved on to become a miner. I doubt if he would have called himself prosperous, other than owning a small miner's cottage and, later in life, the occasional new car, polished and immaculately maintained.

My aunt and her family emigrated from northern Italy, to work in coal mines on the BC side of the Crowsnest Pass. Despite the multiple booms and busts, uncaring mine owners, often dishonest mine bosses, worker strikes that turned violent, minimal safety standards, no benefits and being unable to hang her laundry outside except for Sundays for the coal dust, she remained fatalistically optimistic about new mine openings. She would have cheered on the recently proposed Grassy Mountain mine.

Without alternatives, my uncle and aunt were trapped in the spiral of unsustainable and ephemeral promises of coal. They had coal in their veins and coal on the brain – they were perhaps unable to assess the reality of their situation and envision another future.

My uncle was an angler and a hunter, both pursuits that tune one's observational powers. Yet he never commented on the Crowsnest River turning black with coal fines in the spring or after every rainstorm. He participated in but never acknowledged the decline, collapse and eventual extirpation of bull trout from the upper Crowsnest watershed. The loss of bighorn sheep from Grassy Mountain, a consequence of early mountaintop coal strip mining, never registered even though he toiled in the underground mine beneath the mountain and hunted its slopes on his days off.

No one, including him, would have discerned the invisible contaminants and toxins liberated from the caprock over the coal and flushed downstream. If my uncle and others were concerned about the changes to the landscape, the eroding coal spoil piles, the dust, despoiled rivers and streams, they said nothing.

As Upton Sinclair observed, "It is difficult to get a man to understand something, when his salary depends on his not understanding it." I can't fault my uncle's silence. In contrast to Erasmus's admonishment that "in the land of the blind, a one-eyed man is king," one who can see is treated as a heretic who needs to be silenced, shouted down and discredited by the blind mob.

Coal mining has costs, and they occur at multiple levels – at a human level, a community level and a landscape level, as well as politically, economically and ecologically. We can't, or shouldn't, remain blind to this reality. When we get beyond the boosterism and hype to do a proper accounting, it becomes clear the costs outweigh the benefits. Repeatedly, taxpayers bear the costs, especially the ecological ones, and corporations escape with the benefits while a dumbfounded set of politicians won't own up to being suckered.

Ironically, it is the mine workers who also end up cheated, led on by the boosters, lured into jobs that may not last and often suffering health-related illnesses that could rob them of a long life.

I never asked my uncle if he would have preferred another occupation, maybe farming, where despite the financial risks and the small rewards he could have sidestepped the possibility of violent injury or death. He could have worked in sunlight rather than the glow of a miner's lamp, in fresh air, all the while being his own boss. Maybe he didn't sense he had a choice. We do, and it doesn't involve digging huge holes in the Eastern Slopes.

My uncle's silence on the costs and inevitability of coal mining fortunately doesn't have to pass to us. That was then. In light of history and better information we can be smart enough to not get sucked into a vortex of economic hype, unrealistic promises and destroyed landscapes. We need to pause and ask our politicians to pause and carefully consider the costs and consequences of trying to resurrect a coal mining economy, to liquidate one asset at the expense of so many others. This is not an issue to be complacent about.

In Alberta, the three existing metallurgical coal mines are under "care and maintenance," meaning they are essentially shut down. Alberta mines have gone broke, reclamation bonds proved insufficient and royalties are meagre, throwing a considerable financial burden onto taxpayers. That should tell us something about the reliability of economic forecasts for coal and uncertainties in markets.

Recent evaluations of three BC metallurgical coal mines found the rosy projections for jobs, royalty payments and economic benefits were vastly overstated. Given these circumstances, why any government would promote new coal mine development is a mystery.

A long legacy of environmental failures in all phases of coal development – exploration, mining and reclamation – especially in mountain and foothill landscapes, should make even the most optimistic of us question if it is ever technically feasible to mine coal and protect water quality, species at risk, recreation attributes or other, more sustainable land uses in physically challenging topography.

It would be instructive, and should be mandatory, for our government to conduct a comprehensive survey of all mines in Alberta to capture what was said in initial impact assessments, versus what actually happened, as a guide for future decisions on coal development. The bright light of truth would be a good antidote to the impulse to fall, once more, for a new litany of unrealized and empty promises.

It appears right-wing governments have coal in their veins and coal clogging their brains. If we are to proceed with the fantasy of coal as our economic salvation, all coal development proposals should be vetted through joint federal/provincial hearings to ensure no area of federal responsibility is missed, like protection of species at risk. This might also be an essential curb on current political short-sightedness and economic myopia.

As citizens with a social and ecological conscience, we would do well to express, forcefully, to politicians seemingly in the pocket of foreign companies a singular truth: we've seen enough now to know that our economic salvation doesn't lie with blasting the tops off mountains, burying valleys (and native trout) in overburden, turning our drinking water toxic and contributing to the same human health issues that killed my uncle.

For such truth is, now so clearly, self-evident.

## A VALENTINE FOR ALBERTA'S NORTHERN FOOTHILLS

Remember the kid in school who never got a valentine card? Maybe that child was unfamiliar, from somewhere far away, or just different and distant in some way. It strikes me the Foothills Natural Region (and adjoining pieces of the Boreal Forest Natural Region) of Alberta is like that child.

The northern foothills stretch roughly from Rocky Mountain House to Grande Prairie, with islands into the boreal region. The wedge shape of the foothills back onto the Rocky Mountains and thrust into the boreal. They lie, out of sight, perhaps out of mind for most of Alberta's population who live in more southerly regions. The foothills actually hide in plain sight, spreading over almost 10 per cent of the province. They cover an area bigger than Nova Scotia but seem to command much less respect.

Within the natural area boundaries flow portions of the Peace, Athabasca and North Saskatchewan watersheds, draining north to the Arctic Ocean and east to Hudson Bay. A lot of it is water – big rivers, thousands of smaller tributary streams and a profusion of lakes, ponds, sloughs, wetlands and muskeg. Those who know the foothills and adjacent boreal refer to these landscapes as the "mud, moose and mosquito" biome.

There are few paved highways, and many more gravel and dirt roads that can turn into a morass of mud within hours of a rainstorm. The general lack of familiarity, maybe empathy, with this immense region comes from the lack of easy access.

I have seen portions through the bubble of helicopters, from canoes, and by forays on existing roads. My last exposure was from a commercial flight to Grande Prairie on, of all days, Valentine's. What I saw from a high altitude was disturbing, not at all in keeping with the sentiment of the day.

As far as I could see, for the better part of an hour-long flight, was a profusion of cutlines, roads, pipelines, power lines, logging clear-cuts, wellsites and other industrial installations, one after another, intersecting, overlapping, all jumbled together in an incoherent pattern. Where a moose would find safe haven seemed up for debate.

From the air it looked very much like a demented Etch A Sketch artist went berserk with lines, squares, rectangles and blobs. A less charitable description would be a battle zone, where opposing forces have squared off in a war of subjugation of the natural landscape. Anyone with access to Google Earth might take a similar trip, but seeing it in real time is gut-wrenching. When clouds blotted out the scene on the ground I was momentarily relieved!

I wondered, gazing at the level of disturbance, if we need a new name, and one more accurate, to describe the foothills landscape. Something like the Pillaged Lands, the Tortured Lands or the Scab Lands.

If this is an example of "orderly" resource development, I cringe at what disorder might resemble. It is a bizarre cookie-cutter of industrial development – a remanufacturing of a natural landscape in a blink of time as short as 20 years, according to regional experts.

There is so much of a human footprint you cannot in good conscience always call the landscape "forested." Yes, there are still trees, but the mark of industry overwhelms what was intact forest and watersheds. I struggle to remember that all of this disturbance was done according to some prevailing policy, development rules and regulatory oversight. I sense approvals for most developments were rubber-stamped with no serious oversight.

Today's land-use footprint is a function of ad hoc planning – one wellsite, one road, one logging cutblock at a time without a reckoning of the previous developments and certainly not with a sense of cumulative effects. No overarching regional plan exists for the foothills, despite government of Alberta promises for a land-use framework that date back to 2008.

Regional land-use plans were expected to set the tone for how development would unfold on the landscape, with a sense of environmental considerations (including ecological thresholds) and social expectations, as well as economic drivers. Partly aspirational, partly prescriptive, in theory they would have directed sub-regional planning to take care of the details.

Unfortunately there seems to be little appetite or motivation, along with a lack of capacity and capability, for planning, despite the continued growth of a largely unplanned and chaotic industrial landscape.

The Alberta Biodiversity Monitoring Institute (ABMI), an arm's length, not-for-profit scientific organization, has assessed the extent of the human footprint in Alberta and assembled the findings in a 2017 report, *The Status of Human Footprint in Alberta*. The empirical measurement for the foothills confirms my observations, and is striking – almost a third, 31.2 per cent, of this region has an already existing human footprint. Most of it is from logging, with energy development a close second.

The Grassland and Aspen Parkland Natural Regions have higher degrees of a human footprint, mostly from agriculture. But those footprints have developed over nearly one and a half centuries, compared with less than a 60-year span for the foothills. According to ABMI the footprint in the foothills, led by logging, nearly doubled in an 18-year period (1999–2017). This does not equate to restraint, stewardship or being in the broader public interest.

The foothills are, in large part, an economic generator for Alberta. Timber, conventional oil and gas (with a reliance on fracking), and coal provide rents, royalties and leases. I get that, but to abandon any sort of land-use planning, to avoid setting the direction and the extent of development, to avoid assessing the gains and the losses while not providing the ecological guidelines, including assessment of cumulative effects, seems cavalier and reckless.

Yes, there is an argument that our lifestyles are materially improved by the industrialization of the foothills. But could it have been done differently without sacrificing iconic species like caribou, Athabasca rainbow trout, Arctic grayling and bull trout? Declines in habitat availability and quality have been measured or predicted for every indicator species for biodiversity. The presence, or absence, of these species is a test of our skill, or ineptitude, at managing these lands.

We are repeatedly told, or it is intimated by politicians and corporate spin doctors, that the loss of biodiversity, of landscape intactness, resilience and integrity is the price of progress. We need not mourn these losses considering the economic largesse achieved through excessive development.

But I wonder, what did we sacrifice to create all that black ink in the province's ledger? Did we have to extract all the wealth of the foothills (and continue to do so) so quickly? It is a truism, rarely heeded, that paper capital comes from natural capital, and the latter isn't endless.

If there were a logarithm for stupidity, it would be directly proportional to the square of one's velocity. Applied to land use, it is the speed of development beyond which there is a lapse of reason into greed on a scale proportional to the relative increase in the industrial footprint. Our frantic pace of development in the foothills can only be called stupid.

Sustainable economic development isn't just about sustaining development. It needs to be more in line with public good/public benefits, as well as ecological limits and thresholds, rather than the "get rich quick" schemes and the traditions of corporate wealth at public expense.

To demonstrate and celebrate history, culture and accomplishments, public administrations create monuments of all sorts. What monuments should Alberta erect in honour of the foothills – statues immortalizing end pit lakes, abandoned oil and gas wells, dead rivers, eroding logged areas or a strangling road network? Maybe more enduring monuments could include intact or restored landscapes with thriving caribou populations, lots of native fish and living rivers.

Before we change the rest of the foothills into a fragmented, disconnected and ruined landscape, we need to resurrect land-use planning – cautionary plans for development that invoke stewardship of shared resources. It's unclear why we can't make that step and do so in a timely way, but maybe the answer politically and from corporate centres is (and paraphrasing a line in the movie *Blazing Saddles*) – "Plans? We don't need no stinking plans!"

The foothills deserve a valentine, because we haven't shown them much love! It's going to take more than flowers and chocolate to regain our role as stewards of the treasure that was the foothills.

## HOW MANY GRIZZLY BEARS CAN DANCE ON THE HEAD OF A PIN?

Try to imagine the spirited debates the theologians of old had about how many angels could dance on the head of a pin. Angels no longer dominate today's debates – it is now how many grizzly bears (or sage-grouse, westslope cutthroat trout, caribou and so on) can or do exist on the pinhead of landscape left. Every regulatory hearing to determine the fate of one of those pinheads provides an opportunity for this debate. The panel members, the new theologians, are faced with the ever-present conundrum of balancing environmental protection with economic aspiration.

Our bright academic minds offer a dismal prognosis for the future of healthy landscapes and wildlife. Biologists are worried because populations of many species dip to the point of questionable viability for the future. Westslope cutthroat trout were once so numerous that two anglers, in 1903, caught 400 from Fish Creek in a single day. Fish Creek, which flows through Calgary, now barely merits its name, as with so many streams that once held a cornucopia of native trout. And on it goes.

Alternatively, you could sit through some of the many regulatory hearings that address the parcelling out of Alberta's landscape and resources. The environmental assessments will have a maddening similarity. "Yes, there will be impacts but all can be mitigated. Any residual effect will be so insignificant that the project most assuredly is in the public interest and must proceed. Trust us, we'll monitor the situation and rectify any concerns."

You might be inclined to ask, at the end of these, if the projects are as benign as advertised, the mitigation so effective and the monitoring so conclusive, why aren't we up to our armpits in grizzlies, caribou, sage-grouse or cutthroat trout? We aren't, of course, and it shows the debates, like those of the ancient theologians involving angels, have had little impact on outcomes for species and spaces at risk.

You can see a grizzly in a zoo. A little snippet of the DNA of a westslope cutthroat trout could be held on ice, against a day we might recreate it. But, without place, without the surroundings, without the earth, the wind, the water and the context, we will effectively lose these creatures, and others. We are losing them because we don't grasp the context of species maintenance.

The context is space, big space, appropriate space and un-adulterated space – space without most of the footprint of us. David Brower, of the Sierra Club, eloquently described the California condor, a species teetering on the edge, as 5 per cent flesh, blood, bone and feather – the rest, he said, is place. I would add that place without space is no place at all.

John Weaver, a carnivore biologist, touched on this with his exquisite haiku:

Space is air
For the great beasts who roam the earth
Now is their final breath

There are not many places on this Earth where the wild is still as close at hand as it is in Alberta. Within an easy day's drive of Calgary and Lethbridge are the headwaters of the Old-man and Bow rivers, home to grizzly bears, wolves, cutthroat trout and enough other wildlife to make visitors to our country green with envy. Part of the reason for this expression of bio-logical diversity is the relative ecological intactness of parts of these areas. But there are few remaining areas in the southern foothills where the human footprint is almost non-existent.

What is sad is that the qualities of these landscape jewels, for wildlife and watershed, can slip through our fingers in a heartbeat, with one new human disturbance. It's like the Cheshire cat in *Alice in Wonderland* that "vanished quite slowly, beginning with the end of the tail, and ending with the grin, which remained some time after the rest of it had gone." Many spaces and species are just rudimentary smiles now, remnants of their former glory. That loss started with an off-highway vehicle trail, a road, a logging cutblock or a pipeline and more human traffic.

If something worse could be imagined than losing something, it must be to forget that something was lost. We are perilously close to that point with many Alberta species and their spaces. We are there because we have lost or misplaced our navigational aids to chart changes.

We think the landscape and resources of today is the "full pie." It's part of our combined arrogance and ignorance. The reality is today's pie is a mere slice of yesterday's pie. And without an appreciation of the progressive thinning of the remaining slice it, can, and does, eventually wink out of existence.

We need the same spaces as grizzlies, caribou and cutthroat trout need. It's not because we live there but because these spaces contribute to where we live. Watershed values, storing carbon, preserving possibilities, forming benchmarks and retaining places rich in biodiversity where we can find joy, surprise and humility are of greater importance, arguably, than some of our current resource extraction endeavours.

Others have learned the lesson – let's not be blind to the possibilities of change while the options stare us in the face. A seemingly altruistic act of saving imperilled spaces and species now may be viewed shortly as a perfectly reasonable, selfish act to save ourselves. You see, it's also us up there, dancing the Macarena on that pinhead.

### STUCK IN THE MUD
*The OHV Debate*

———

As Yogi Berra said, "You can observe a lot by just watching." Observing off-highway vehicle (OHV) users reveals much about the attitudes and beliefs of the group. One picks up some notable conclusions.

OHV users actually seem to believe they can be trusted as stewards of the land by criss-crossing it with spinning tires; denying the scientific evidence of OHV impacts, absolving themselves of blame; advancing their interests over those of other users, inventing lies, distortions and "fake" news; and answering differing opinions with slurs, threats and intimidation. It's hard not to conclude that the OHV community is at war with reasonable and rational citizens.

OHV users have a loose relationship with facts, including false beliefs about generally accepted science and a propensity to use misinformation to further cloud the issues. Their opinions seem not to change, even after falsehoods are corrected. The question is why.

Finding facts, pursuing evidence, keeping an open mind and trusting science is part of my background. Science keeps us alive, makes life easier, entertains us and helps with problem solving. Science isn't perfect, but it sure beats ignorance. It isn't clear to me how ignoring it advances anyone's cause.

Denying science findings about the effects of OHV use on fish, wildlife and water quality is exactly the same as suggesting the sun rotates around the Earth or the Earth is flat. In letters and comments, OHV users keep denying that wildlife is impacted by their activity. Yet a recent summary of 700 research papers clearly shows the impacts. Would 50 or 100 more research studies convince disbelievers?

Similarly, OHV users contend fish aren't harmed by sediment created by erosion from their vehicles. Over 50 years of careful research indicates that fish are impacted in profoundly negative ways by sediment. It is doubtful another 50 years of research would demonstrate any different conclusion.

OHV users respond to scientific evidence like the early English tourist to Africa, on seeing a giraffe for the first time – "I see it, but I still do not believe it." Many choose to deny the science on OHV impacts, deny the relevance of that science to management actions and simply vilify those who report on the science.

No one can boast of good stewardship who chooses not to understand and accept the evidence of ecological science. Knowledge provides the map to navigate to an appropriate destination. Its absence has a lot to do with all the mudholes out there.

A recurring comment from OHV users is that they care about the environment. If OHV users will not accept scientific evidence, how can they assert an honest care for a shared environment? The tragedy of the effects of OHV use on wildlife is not found in the facts of the situation, but in the failure of the OHV community to respond to the facts, except with dismissal.

What the OHV community says is they want to be good, responsible stewards of the land. Their words betray a different motive – to perpetuate their recreational activity regardless of the cost to land, other users or society as a whole.

Another disturbing bit of OHV propaganda is that putting some restrictions on unbridled OHV use isn't really about protecting Alberta's watersheds, fish and wildlife, and restoring the chance for quiet recreationalists to enjoy public land. Instead, it's described as social engineering – a denial of basic human rights and freedoms and the end of all public use.

The OHV users blame a cabal of left-wing extremist environmental groups funded from secret US sources – so secret, apparently, that they don't show up on the financial reports environmental groups regularly submit to Revenue Canada and make available for public review. This is a remarkable effort to replace reasoned debate with a muddy brew of conspiracy theory, right-wing populism and anti-government invective.

Mark Twain is reported as saying, "A lie is halfway round the world before the truth has got its boots on" (although Jonathan Swift may have coined the expression). And a lie, no matter how many times it is repeated, is just that, a lie. Indeed, the OHV community seems to derive its support from principles in Aunt Jobiska's Theorem (from Edward Lear), "It's a fact the whole world knows," as well as the Bellman's Theorem (from Lewis Carroll), "What I tell you three times is true."

Some in the OHV group even resort to childhood tactics like name calling, trying to hide the weakness of their position by demeaning others. Grown-ups don't do this. It destroys any chance of coherence, civility and cooperation.

One final observation. The anarchy, lawlessness and destruction that is motorized recreation will come to an end. Albertans are increasingly fed up with it. Yet, letters to the editor in many Alberta newspapers and virulent Facebook rants suggest that the OHV community has chosen rage over reason. If these people and their organizations are the best spokespeople available for OHV use, they are not just a threat to our public lands; they are showing themselves to be their own worst enemy.

• CHAPTER 5 •

## THE MYTH OF ALBERTA
## ENVIRONMENTAL EXCEPTIONALISM

———

Alberta is portrayed in tourism marketing materials with sweeping, pristine landscapes and the pronouncement "Remember to breathe." At the same time, the province is advertised as "open for business." To ensure that environmentally conscious investors are not put off, a picture is painted of high regulatory standards and social licence. It would seem we in Alberta are at the pinnacle of environmental excellence.

The province and right-wing politicians proclaim, "Our energy sector is the most responsible energy sector across the planet, [and] has the highest environmental, social and government standards." This isn't the first time we've heard those words and it likely won't be the last. Others have used the time-worn phrase "world-class" to describe Alberta's environmental standards.

I am unaware of any independent, arms-length confirmation of these assertions. Ironically, exceptionalism is touted in every part of the world. Every claim to be exceptional disproves itself because of insularity. Governments can be the purveyors of grand myths, and few are as insidious as those portraying Alberta's environmental exceptionalism. To be clear, the myth may not have been invented here, but Alberta seems to have taken out a patent on it and its wholesale use.

Politicians have become strident cheerleaders for unparalleled development, blindly championing the industries that destabilize us politically, socially and environmentally. They are intent on navigating (and maybe circumventing or erasing) the regulatory hurdles put in place by previous, more careful administrations. They create illusionary boxes of oversight to be checked off in order to assure a positive spin for resource extraction and exploitation.

This is done under a rallying cry of "getting Alberta back to work," drowning out the true motive for unwinding environmental protection tools, which is simply to increase economic returns. The unmistakeable signal from politicians is that environmental protection policies and legislation are frivolous and impede economic recovery. This is the essence of their campaign of "red tape" reduction.

Words, as any lawyer will attest, are slippery. They can convey, initially, a feeling of understanding, of shared meaning and a minimizing of concerns. I would agree Alberta has higher standards than say, Venezuela, Russia or Nigeria, but what does that really mean? If you fudge the standards or fail to properly define them, the ideal of standards falls away and becomes meaningless.

Politicians and corporate leaders chant about excellence in environmental standards, hoping to drown out the sounds of unpleasant revelations. Catchy slogans are a preferred tool.

Consider this slogan: "Clean coal." What a righteous ring it has. It summons the aura of a wholesome, immaculate substance. But stripping away the layers, as happens in the mining of coal, shows it is neither clean, immaculate nor wholesome.

"Clean" is not a word one should associate with mountaintop removal, selenium contamination, global warming, acute and chronic human health issues, loss of threatened trout species, wildlife disruption, siltation of streams, sediment pond failures, coal dust migrating miles downwind, noise and an economic bust that inevitably follows the mining boom. Tacking on the adjective "clean" fails miserably to enhance the virtue or dismiss the effects of coal mining.

We need to be very skeptical of what any government, the Coal Association of Canada, or coal companies tell us about the merits of "clean" coal mining, especially in our headwaters.

In the Eastern Slopes, coal is closest to the surface on mountaintops and hence, more economical to extract. These are also the headwaters for many Albertans, and the streams harbour several species of imperilled native trout.

This creates an issue for wildlife like bighorn sheep, who use these areas as critical winter range and secure lambing areas, and species like bull trout and westslope cutthroat trout, both requiring clean, sediment-free water.

This seems to have escaped the notice of the Alberta Energy Regulator (AER), the agency responsible for regulating, in the public interest, any industrial activity. On several occasions now, foreign-owned coal companies have been given major variances, allowing incursion into these areas within critical time periods, voiding any sense of fish and wildlife protection. Permission to do so has occurred seemingly within minutes of receiving the company's requests, suggesting an unusual level of clairvoyance on the part of the regulator.

Statements of concern from environmental organizations have been dismissed with a classic "Catch-22" response that the concerns could not be registered because approvals had already been provided. As the environmental community points out, "It seems that to participate in the AER's process one must be able to anticipate when companies will submit applications and submit a statement of concern before the application is posted online publicly." Maybe the clairvoyants in AER can tell us how this can be done.

Another slogan is "ethical oil." Despite this slogan's feel-good message, "ethical oil" has not been shown to produce lower greenhouse gas (GHG) emissions. Even reducing the amount of GHG emissions per barrel of oil has little relevance to environmental excellence if the number of barrels produced continues to increase.

It is now clear from federal government research that gas leaks (fugitive emissions), especially those of methane gas, are a very potent GHG. These emissions are alarmingly high from Alberta gas wells and facilities. Monitoring and regulatory oversight have been shown to be insufficient to even assess the magnitude of the issue, let alone deal with the suppression of these leaks.

Appending the word "ethical" to the product of the petroleum industry hasn't prevented the abandonment of thousands of wells with insufficient reclamation bonds and the reality that taxpayers will have to foot the bills for cleanup. It also hasn't solved the need to clean up and restore oilsands mines with substantial, unfunded financial liabilities and no clear strategies for effective remediation.

There is no slogan to sanctify lumber produced in Alberta, similar to "clean coal" and "ethical oil," but if there were it might be "immaculate logs" or "laundered lumber."

The boreal mixed wood and the Eastern Slopes forests are subject to the pressure of cumulative effects, and the largest human footprint is logging. Clear-cuts change the hydrologic regime, increasing the speed and magnitude of runoff. Skid trails and roads capture runoff and deliver water and sediment faster to receiving streams. Poorly installed culverts block upstream fish passage. Herbicide treatment to suppress deciduous trees, in favour of conifers, changes the mosaic of natural forests, including essential riparian vegetation.

Several independent cumulative effects assessments have shown that many other forest values – biodiversity, water quality and recreation – cannot be maintained under current levels of timber harvest. A 2020 cumulative effects report commissioned by the Alberta Chapter of The Wildlife Society, a group of professional biologists, academics and consultants, was dismissed by the UCP government, with the response that the department was already using "adaptive and sustainable forest management." The minister in charge of Alberta's forests called on his officials instead to increase logging exponentially to boost economic activity. This isn't forest management – this is timber mining.

Of the five salmonid species native to the streams and rivers of watersheds subject to logging, one species, Athabasca rainbow trout, is considered Endangered. Two species, bull trout and westslope cutthroat trout, have been designated Threatened. Arctic grayling is a "species of special concern," and mountain whitefish are deemed "secure" even though their populations have crashed in many watersheds. This is not an expression of successful "adaptive and sustainable forest management."

Logging is also implicated in the drastic decline of caribou populations. Only two of Alberta's identified herds of caribou are deemed "stable," whatever that term means. Some no longer exist. Most herds are plummeting, with population graphs that resemble playground slides. Herds are now largely isolated from one another on diminishing islands of habitat. All we are left with is a very strong sense that caribou are in a slow race to oblivion in Alberta. Maintaining the land-use status quo, especially timber harvest, means the elimination of caribou in a relatively short time frame.

How did we get here?

We're at this point because our political leaders have focused on economic development at the expense of all other values. Instead of meaningfully balancing development with environmental protection, we get face-saving, empty slogans without substance or effective governance.

Alberta might well be "exceptional" – but not for the reasons we had hoped. Right-wing governments seem determined to turn our Eastern Slopes, the source of water for the majority of Albertans, into a series of black holes flanked by a toxic chemical stew, and convert our forests into stumps and muddy off-highway vehicle trails. In the boreal mixed woods, there will be little slackening of logging despite the spectre of caribou disappearing.

Greenhouse gas emissions will increase, and our world will become warmer, with more extreme weather events that will challenge food production, our safety and our ability to pay the costs of increased liability. And the aftermath of oilsands mining will be an enduring and expensive toxic legacy. Yes, this is exceptional. Shameful but exceptional.

Obfuscating profit-driven intentions with a false narrative about Alberta environmental exceptionalism is disgraceful. We can do so much better than this, with transparency, humility, honesty and ethical behaviour. We should aspire to environmental exceptionalism in Alberta, but we won't achieve it with empty slogans.

## TWO FISH, ONE FISH, NO FISH
### *Alberta's Fish Crisis*

————

Dr. Seuss's *One Fish Two Fish Red Fish Blue Fish* is a classic children's story, a simple rhyming book for beginning readers. We need a similar rhyme to help people grasp the problems afflicting Alberta's native fish species. It might read like this:

> Two fish, one fish, dead fish, no fish,
> No grayling or goldeye, something's amiss.
> This one's got a tumor and a rotten fin,
> There's no home for that one to live in,
> Say, what a lot of fish there used to be,
> Where are the fish for my kid and me?

My apologies to Dr. Seuss, but what would he have thought of the sorry state of fish in Alberta? Would he have said, "From there to here, from here to there, funny things are everywhere"? His words could have been prophetic: the funny things are actually very sad little tragedies that have morphed into a province-wide decline in fish abundance, distribution, diversity and health. As with convicts on death row, trends indicate dead fish swimming, where populations have been driven to perilously low levels.

The current status of fish populations cannot be appreciated until we acknowledge where we were by reviewing historical abundance and distribution. Only then will we grasp where we are and be ready to see the losses and the potential for recovery.

Lost on the awareness of most Albertans are the missing fish. At best these fish are ghosts, apparitions of past times, rarely remembered and easily forgotten. At worst they are thought to have never existed.

It is sad, but fish just don't live here anymore. It was not always so for fish, and the slide started long before Alberta became a province.

Fish were once a staple in the diet of Indigenous Peoples and those in the fur industry, especially in the parkland and boreal forest regions. David Thompson, the Hudson's Bay Company surveyor, fur trader and mapmaker, wrote in the late 18th century, "When a new trading House is built...everyone is anxious to know the quality of the fish it contains for whatever it is they have they have no other[food] for the winter." The daily ration at the post at Fort Chipewyan was four fish and one potato.

In 1798 a Hudson's Bay Company post was established on Lac La Biche. Lac La Biche is a big, shallow and productive lake located in the boreal forest northeast of Edmonton. Thirteen species of fish inhabited the lake, obviously in substantial numbers that encouraged first Indigenous settlement and then establishment of fur trading posts. During the first year David Thompson recorded their nets caught northern pike, lake whitefish, walleye and white suckers that the inhabitants of the post happily consumed. By 1819 lake whitefish constituted the main menu item of the post.

In her doctoral thesis, Dr. Andrea McGregor painstakingly quantified the harvest of fish from Lac La Biche that supported the westward expansion of the fur trade and settlement. The annual harvest of lake whitefish increased from 85 tons caught in 1800 to over 1,200 tons in 1875. But even subsistence harvest by a relatively small population was not sustainable and the fishery collapsed in 1878.

Memories are short, and 34 years later, apparently undaunt-
ed by previous fisheries failures, commercial fishing was introduced as an industry in 1912, shifting business from fur to
fish. A rail line was extended to the lake in 1915, and by 1918
200 commercial fishermen were harvesting and processing lake
whitefish, cisco, walleye and pike. Just as the subsistence fishery
proved unsustainable, so too did the commercial one.

As the Depression of the 1930s hit, paradoxically the market
for fur escalated. This drove demand for fish for mink ranching. Although the target was the cisco population (a diminutive
relative of the lake whitefish), small mesh gill nets unselectively
caught large numbers of perch, walleye, pike and lake whitefish.
It is thought this was a crippling blow to the sustainability of
the walleye population.

To add indignity to the injury of overfishing, by the 1950s the
essential watershed integrity that supported the lake and its fish
populations had been compromised. Excessive nutrients delivered from human changes in the watershed and from lakeshore
developments provided too much of a good thing to an already
productive, eutrophic lake.

Insult followed indignity, and by 1970 walleye had effectively
been extirpated and by the 1990s pike and perch populations
had declined dramatically. The finny wealth of lake whitefish
that encouraged settlement has been reduced to a fraction of
historic levels.

Attempts to resuscitate the walleye population have gone
on for some decades, including massive stocking of fry, derived
from stock from other lakes. Re-establishing a predator like walleye has some challenges. In an ironic twist, yellow perch, a prey
item in adult walleye diets, eat large numbers of young walleye

fry. Without a critical mass of adult walleye to reduce the perch population, the prey species bites back hard on the predator.

Time will tell if walleye can be re-established at some ecologically relevant level. Dr. McGregor suggests that the failure of the lake whitefish population to rebound over the last 50 years is a systemic result of possibly irreversible changes in the lake ecosystem. We've influenced the ecological cogs and wheels of the lake's delicate mechanism, tipped the balance too far and the lake may not have the capability to snap back to some previous steady state.

David Thompson would not be impressed.

In fishing-dominated circles great debates rage. It is usually over whether or not a fish population is declining or increasing. Opinions are usually strong, though somewhat unsubstantiated by fact, and there is little wiggle room for compromise in the conversations. Experts are numerous on both sides.

Just when the evidence seems to indicate in favour of a dwindling population, someone catches a big one and fuel is added to the fire of debate. While the angler responds to how many were caught and their size, the tools of fisheries science are more sophisticated and can tell a different story about the status of a fish population.

It is probably human nature that we are more inclined to listen for the bang of things going seriously, quickly and irrevocably wrong, but tend to be deaf to the whisper, the whimper of the incremental pathway to the same endpoint.

There are theories of extinctions of the geological past that center on asteroids – massive, external events that precipitated a cataclysmic, catastrophic demise of creatures. Then there have been the human-induced extirpations and extinctions, including a large part of the postglacial megafauna of North America, the dodo bird, right whales, the passenger pigeon and the bison. The last one, bison, probably still resonates in most minds.

But it goes on. Only the scope and scale differ, and in the case of native fish, not by much. What is different is that the retreat of fish is a largely silent, unseen and unheralded event. Fish are not only out of sight; they are out of mind. This is the modern version of the bison demise played out on an aquatic stage behind a watery curtain that is opaque at best.

Theoretically, fish species missing or in decline enjoyed some statutory safety, at least from angler harvest, but the watersheds that sustained them have limited protection. There is "intentional harm" – poaching fish, for example. There is also "incidental harm" that alters habitat in ways that impair life cycle requirements – like sediment bleeding from logging roads. Most critically, if habitat is not being protected, things will not improve for fish.

In another Dr. Seuss children's story is found this: "So, open your mouth, lad! For every voice counts!" Native fish need acknowledgement, empathy, encouragement and friends. Otherwise the rhyme will continue as:

> Over in the meadow where the stream ran blue,
> Lived an old mother fish and her little fishes two.
> Dug and cut and dumped did we.
> So much money in our pockets, see.
> Then there were none where there used to be two.
> Fish used to live where the stream ran blue.

## WHAT HAPPENED TO ALL OF ALBERTA'S FISH?

Stories of the cornucopia of Alberta's former fish resources are legion. My sister-in-law recalls her father, of Icelandic origins, harvesting sacks of fish from several Medicine River tributaries in the 1940s and early 1950s. They were likely pike and suckers and were ground up to make fish cakes. Sometimes the grinding didn't completely break down the bones, producing an unwelcome surprise when eaten.

Today, it is difficult to find water in these streams, let alone fish. We are resigned to eating fish sticks from ocean stocks without ever realizing what we've lost from our own backyards.

Now, just about everywhere you look there might be memories, but few or no fish. Maybe, when you lose the memory, you lose the fish. So, what happened to those bounteous finny resources?

The simple answer is – we killed them. This may not mean that was the desired outcome or that we meant for it to happen. We may not have been aware of the consequences of our actions, and we might have firmly believed more fish existed.

The longer answer to what happened to all those fish is a bit more difficult. To get at the answer we need to examine what's meant when it's said, "Fish are harvested." The phrase means much more than the obvious – the fish caught and kept by anglers and commercial fishers. We also harvest fish by the ways we develop, the ways we exploit, the ways we use landscapes. Simply put, every land-use decision has a consequence for fish.

Each unit of aquatic habitat, the sum of appropriate water quality, quantity and temperature along with abundant overhead and instream cover, clean substrate and riparian shading, is capable of producing and sustaining a number of units of fish. Any activity that degrades or eliminates units of habitat effectively "harvests" fish because it removes the potential for fish to exist.

A fish removed from the water on the end of a fishing line may die sooner, but death is just as inevitable when fish habitat is altered, compromised or destroyed. The difference is that removing a fish by angling usually has minimal impact on the viability of the population. Lost habitat eliminates not only the existing fish but also any hope for population recovery.

Farmers, miners, off-highway vehicle users, roughnecks, homeowners, politicians and a cast of thousands have devastated Alberta's fish populations without ever catching, let alone frying, a single fish. Instead, large numbers of fish, populations of fish and watersheds of fish were killed through habitat alterations, loss of critical habitats, water withdrawals and pollution. Alberta's fish have died by a thousand cuts, not a thousand hooks.

Fish losses in Alberta are not solely an artifact of history – it's a current event, happening as you read this, in a watershed near you. The past has an annoying way of trespassing into the present. Every decision about how we use and develop land, water and other resources is a decision about the fate of fish. And the myth of endless growth and the policy of multiple use without weighing the consequences of either mindset have sentenced many fish to an untimely end.

What's the prognosis for Alberta's native fish and what can be done about population declines?

With a few tiny exceptions, movement towards actively managing or restoring fish habitat is glacial in speed. The provincial government's *Fish Conservation and Management Strategy for Alberta* contains good words on integration, planning, monitoring, use of science and stewardship to benefit fish. But it is weak on the crucial issue of implementation. It doesn't demand enough actions that would ultimately produce and sustain fish by protecting and restoring habitat.

Since watershed management is the key to keeping fish swimming, everyone involved in land uses and landscape planning must pitch in. Sadly, few understand that their role also includes fish conservation. Fisheries biologists cannot do this on their own since the levers they can pull to effect positive change for fish are limited.

It is all about priorities. There is a consistency in policy that favours economic development over environmental protection. Part of the collateral damage of narrowly focused land-use decisions is the loss of fish. What is noticeably absent is the spine to address the thorny issues of conservation targets and thresholds.

One thing about fishery collapses is that they are not completely predictable and do not happen according to some recipe. All the fish don't usually die at once. Instead, they disappear in a series of almost indistinguishable whimpers, too quietly, too silently for most to notice.

However, we are getting better at defining thresholds – the crucial lines that, once crossed, signal imminent fish population collapse. Sediment from an eroding human land-use footprint has long been recognized as a mortal threat for fish. The relationship between road density, the land-use footprint, sediment and fish population persistence (or not) seems clear. The research results are exhaustive, categorical and yet unconscionably ignored as our land-use footprint continues to bleed sediment.

The cumulative and, in many cases, irreversible loss of native fish virtually everywhere in Alberta over our history of settlement should shock us. If anything approximating this had happened to most of Alberta's charismatic mammalian species, it likely would have made for banner headlines and some level of political commitment to action.

It is perplexing that this happened in modern times, with some level of environmental consciousness and overlapping government responsibility. It speaks to institutional barriers that preclude action, poor communication between silos in government and a lack of oversight mechanisms. Add a reluctance to regulate and enforce to this daunting list. Mostly it speaks to our failure to plan for tomorrow, to use existing evidence to guide us onto a path of better decisions.

Does the plight of Alberta's fish deserve a call for action?

Fish, given their watery homes, are largely invisible to us air breathers. It isn't that fish are actually invisible; it is that people are unused to seeing them, to perceiving that they live beneath the surface of the water. Of course, if no one sees them, are they really there at all? And, if they somehow disappear, does anyone note their disappearance?

It's this invisibility of fish that makes it too easy to disregard their present plight and the decline in habitat that supports them. It makes it easier to ignore potential and lost capability and set erroneous goals for fisheries management.

As Dr. Andrea McGregor points out about fish slip-sliding away, "Managers, scientists and citizens are likely to assume the ecosystem conditions of the intermediate and distant past resemble those of their own remembered history and thus can be ignored – a classic characteristic of the shifting baseline syndrome."

A question Albertans should answer, before the last fish swims to a watery grave, is this: Shall we be bold and ask for some of the fish harvest back we have lost through habitat losses? To answer *yes* means we will require habitat restoration, riparian revival, fewer chemicals leaking into the water, leaving more water in rivers and less sediment to muddy the water.

The affirmative answer commits us to watershed improvement, true integrated planning, full cost accounting and an ecological approach to decision making about future resource decisions. We need something comprehensive like the Marshall Plan, designed for rebuilding Europe after the Second World War, for fish habitat restoration in Alberta.

Or we could just answer *no* and call this failure to act – as we have become accustomed to do – the price of progress. I hope that, on reflection, we will decide progress sometimes has too high a price tag, especially when applied to fish.

*Illustration by Liz Saunders*

# 6
# Lessons

*That men do not learn very much from the
lessons of history is the most important of all
the lessons that history has to teach.*

—Aldous Huxley

## LEARNING FROM A ROBIN

Snowflakes fell, melted and coalesced on the branches of the spruce tree outside my office window (this was when I was still gainfully employed). Even though by the calendar it was spring, it was a rotten day for nest building. Yet, a female robin paid scant attention and scavenged grass, twigs and often wrappers and other refuse from the pavement of the convenience store next door. Those who litter have no idea of the unintended service they provide.

While the robin assembled nest materials, I stared at my computer screen, trying to make sense of the latest email missive, departmental pronouncement and heart-rending reports on the population status of various species. Mostly I wondered how to massage the latest funding request with the right words to tug at the hearts of those reading it and deliver money to aid wildlife conservation.

Oblivious to me, and all I was trying to do on behalf of wildlife, the robin carried on, a piece of home collected and delivered to the nest site, on average every three to four minutes. She struggled with a clot of tissue paper, almost as large as her. I struggled with program administration, in volume perhaps larger. Her task, driven by biological urges, seemed straightforward. My motivation was a combination of legal, moral and personal responsibility to ensure wild creatures and their habitats weren't lost in a welter of economic aspirations.

Now, robins are humble, practical birds. She had found a reasonable nest site that provided some concealment from the prying eyes and depredations of magpies and crows. Robin nests don't have porches, spiral staircases, cupulas, dormers or even a roof. The nest, unassuming to us humans, was what was needed, and no more. Granted, except for the nesting season, robins don't have a need for a nest. From a variety of vantage points they can chat up the neighbours, eye up the cat and pillage the ripening fruit on the tree across the way, once the family has vacated the nest.

Biologists are made humble by the intricacies and complexities of wildlife conservation. First is understanding the ecology and biology of wild critters. What is their relationship to a variety of habitats, and which ones are essential for survival? What is the tolerance for human disturbance? What fluctuations in populations are natural and which are not? Is there reason for concern?

Determining why a population is in decline is often like attempting to solve a cold-case crime. Many of the clues have been erased or are missing. The witnesses, if there were any, are either gone or their memories too poor to be relied on. In total the evidence is scant, fragmented, and the dots hard to connect, especially when it involves the additive effect of many things slowly accumulating to a tipping point.

The vexing question is when does a downward trend in numbers signal something disturbing, where intervention might be required? Next are the steps of where, when and how to intervene, and with what.

The robin's steps, from collecting materials from the surrounding landscape and melding them into a nest, were relatively simple. Mine were convoluted, time consuming and uncertain of success. She was absolutely focused on her task. We in wildlife conservation often find ourselves distracted and pulled in several directions, away from the course. Our "nests" rarely get built. She could teach us all an important lesson on "focus."

Wildlife, including that industrious robin, is perfectly capable of looking after their needs within the sweep of natural events, including cyclical ebbs and flows. What wildlife cannot cope with is the influence of changes brought on by us humans. Sometimes I think the best thing we could do for wildlife, for their conservation, is to stay out of their way and quit limiting their habitat options.

Given the inventory of what walks, crawls, flies over, swims through or roots itself in Alberta, there is never enough information to provide ironclad proof to convince uninterested politicians, corporate executives with ice water in their veins or a distracted public that they should care. The robin only must worry about herself and her nest. Biologists have many nests of concern.

Yet we both plod on, oblivious to the weather or the challenges. I'm inspired by her efforts, and I returned to my task of administering a conservation program that might, if persistence is the key, benefit some of her wild relatives. I was in doubt that my efforts would have any direct effect on her, whereas she was already motivated by biological imperatives.

In the administration of conservation programs, I am reminded of the question: What is important? Well, it can be one female robin, building a nest in a spruce tree outside an office complex in an urban setting. It's keeping wildlife and the opportunities for wildlife in all corners of our landscapes, urban ones included. It's remembering that computers and convenience stores and conservation programs are all wonderful artifacts of human civilization, but a robin building a nest is a more tangible signal of our relationship with the Earth.

As a postscript to this learning from a robin, the spruce tree that had given it a nesting spot also had become shelter under its spreading branches for homeless people, many afflicted with addictions. That created issues of crime and harassment of the building's legitimate occupants. As is so often the case in such situations, the response is to deal with the problem by shuffling those with the least number of options off somewhere else. This was accomplished by cutting down the tree, an innocent bystander in the affair.

In a way, axing the spruce tree was an apt metaphor for wildlife habitat losses. It was to wildlife as homeless people are to social consciousness – unaccountably overlooked. As in the symmetry with homeless people, often wildlife have few other options for sustaining themselves and finding shelter. The belief that wildlife can simply move is a hollow comfort and an unrealized expectation we use to rationalize taking over their habitats.

It's unlikely the loss of robin habitat was even noticed, yet these little lives are part of a tapestry that connects us to a wider, wilder world. Robins aren't in any danger of disappearing, taking their easily identified song with them. But every time a bit of habitat disappears, we run up a deficit in our stewardship account. This is a bill that grows larger and is mostly unpaid.

Seeing other robins in the city going about their robin business made me ponder the lesson from the one I saw on that raw spring day. To some, wild things may be an insignificant part of their lives. To a few of us, those wild things are a reminder of a place where we want to live.

## THE GRASS THAT CHEATS

There it was, at the US–Canada border, slyly occupying the road margins and sticking up from cracks in the pavement. It had been able to march – uncontrolled, unquestioned and ignored – into Alberta. Ironically, we were stopped and questioned on our re-entry about our nationality, residence, purchases and cash amounts. Border agents were curiously uninterested in the risk of this invasive species, almost under their feet, that undermines our economic and ecological integrity.

Cheatgrass – an almost invisible scourge, an invasive plant, an unwelcome immigrant. It has many aliases, including downy brome and annual brome, but all fit under the Latin handle of *Bromus tectorum*. The descriptor *tectorum* means roof, since in Europe its habitat was the decaying straw of thatched roofs.

We should be wary of a plant that can make a living on the roof of a house.

Cheatgrass is nasty and deceptive. It is well named. Resembling a relationship that starts out full of promise, initially cheatgrass presents luxuriant, green growth. But by about mid-June the growth spurt is done, and the plant senesces, dries up and leaves behind a golden-brown, desiccated and flammable carpet with a prolific seed crop. In Alberta it has earned another appropriate name – "noxious."

Plants are short, standing from ankle height to just below the knee, with a drooping head, like oats. Prickly awns arm each seed. The long, stiff awns easily penetrate the skin in the mouth, throat and intestine of grazing animals, embed themselves in dogs and wildlife, and hitch a free ride in clothing and boots. A year after a canoe trip on the Missouri River in Montana, where the native range has been largely usurped by cheatgrass, I found a seed hidden in the waistband of a pair of underwear.

To deal with arid conditions it grows quickly in the spring, sets large quantities of seed and dies. Seeds germinate in the fall and the plant overwinters as a seedling. The plant is diabolically efficient at extracting moisture from the soil. It has a fast-growing, divided root system that allows it to extract most of the available moisture from the shallow surface layer of the soil profile. Roots of cheatgrass continue to grow at lower temperatures than native plants, allowing it to stake out a site before other plant species establish.

That gives cheatgrass a large competitive advantage, making use of spring melt and nutrients very early in spring, compared to our slower-growing perennial grasses. Plant ecologists refer to its reproductive behaviour as a "big bang" type. Native plants can have a hard time competing with it.

It is an old-world grass that has immigrated to North America, probably using the same dispersal mechanism of that seed in my underwear. Like many immigrants it has prospered, to the point where few places are free of it. Native rangelands and farmlands in the western US have been particularly overrun. Researchers have commented that seldom in recent history has the vegetation of such a large geographic area of the western states been transformed so rapidly and permanently as it has by the invasion and spread of cheatgrass. As with other highly invasive species, the threats for Alberta are chilling.

Fire has been a natural feature of native grasslands, but cheatgrass ups the ante and the risk considerably. Where cheatgrass has dominated and increased densities of dry material, fires are kindled and spread rapidly, with greater size and frequency. More frequent fires reduce the extent of many native grasses, forbs and shrubs, to the detriment of many wildlife species. Fires leave the land vulnerable to erosion and to the continued spread of cheatgrass. Cheatgrass creates the perfect storm of a positive feedback loop.

Cheatgrass thrives on disturbance – overgrazing, roads, paths, industrial developments, cultivation, urban areas, unvegetated waste areas – wherever robust, healthy native plant communities have been compromised. But the frightening part about this plant is that it doesn't need disturbance to secure a beachhead. It can invade intact native rangelands without an open door.

Its spread in Alberta has not been monitored, but anecdotal evidence from ranchers, botanists and range managers suggest cheatgrass is on the march and increasing from beachheads along the US border. Barry Adams, a retired provincial range manager, has noted its spread over less than two decades from the semi-arid southeast corner of Alberta through to the well-watered southwestern corner.

Riparian areas are not immune from the invasion of cheatgrass. Alberta Cows & Fish has a measuring stick for riparian health that blends physical site characteristic with a botanical appraisal. Cheatgrass has been found to be widely distributed in the South Saskatchewan drainage, the Milk River watershed and in cities and towns where riparian assessments have been done.

Climate change may be a factor, since spring rainfall over the last 20 years has been higher. This favours opportunistic invaders like cheatgrass. Dr. Walter Willms, an emeritus federal range scientist, points out that periodic population surges can be triggered by variables like moisture (especially timing), temperature and changes in range conditions. Like an unwelcome house guest who spreads out and takes over, room by room, once established cheatgrass is difficult to evict.

This invader has the potential to cheat ranchers out of late summer and fall forage supply, causes a loss of native plant diversity, with a corresponding negative ripple effect on wildlife, and ratchets up the risk of catastrophic wildfire that will imperil ecosystem functions. Finally, cheatgrass will decrease the pleasure of a grassland romp as the needle-sharp seeds embed themselves in socks, underwear and pets.

Like other invasive species, once cheatgrass gets a toehold it is impossible to eradicate and difficult to control. Maintaining healthy, intact native grasslands is the first line of defence, says Dr. Edward Bork, the Chair of Rangeland Ecology and Management at the University of Alberta.

Chemical and mechanical (mowing) control on disturbed lands, road edges and railroad rights-of-way discourages establishment and spread. One herbicide that inhibits seedlings from establishing is being tested by Anabel Dombro, one of Dr. Bork's graduate students. At trial levels it reduced cheatgrass biomass and density without impacting native plants. A root-colonizing bacterium that inhibits cheatgrass growth shows promise for more widespread control, as tested by the US Department of Agriculture.

Stopping establishment seems key to control. As it's a common contaminant in seed supplies, it's difficult to separate cheatgrass from native grass seed and from cereal grains. Cheatgrass is found, in small quantities, even in "Certified" seed used for reclamation and agricultural crops. There is a tendency on the part of seed growers to downplay the risk of cheatgrass, because more stringent regulations would hamper the economics of the industry. Seeds are also transported on industrial equipment and in hay.

There is consensus in broader circles about the risk posed by cheatgrass for Alberta's native plant communities and those that depend on them. What is still to be determined is the extent of the risk. The impression from those working at ground level is that cheatgrass is most invasive and a major concern in southern Alberta, where it can dominate entire pastures. In the dry south its invasiveness isn't limited by soil or site characteristics, unlike farther north where populations might colonize a site but be less competitive with established plant communities.

Surveillance, immediate control and consistent follow-up are key ingredients to thwarting cheatgrass. But, as in efforts to deal with other invasive species, we fail miserably at these essential actions. History suggests that by the time we recognize the issue, it is often too late to deal with an invasive species in any meaningful way. Cheatgrass is with us, a rank and sturdy weed, and to avoid an economic and ecological catastrophe, we need to respond aggressively.

When ecological integrity isn't regularly and robustly measured and monitored, it is difficult to pinpoint when an invasive species establishes, the extent of its spread and where it tends to dominate the native community. Control measures fail because of a lack of immediate diligence and follow-through. One of the confounding issues with invasive species like cheatgrass is that ecological integrity initially declines imperceptibly, a little worse than yesterday but not noticeable enough to set off alarms.

The ecologist Aldo Leopold said, "One of the penalties of an ecological education is that one lives alone in a world of wounds." Most of the people passing through the border crossing as I did, or walking down most back alleys, or driving along a boulevard or strolling on a park trail, would not see the plant or be able to interpret the consequences of its presence. Things change, sometimes dramatically and irrevocably, when we lack awareness and aren't watching. Sometimes it takes the stab of a prickly awn in the waistband of our underwear to make us pay attention.

## PAINT THE PRAIRIE
### *Blazing Star*

———

From across a drab and desiccated expanse of grassland one can make out a tiny flame, not of a fire, but of the lavender blossoms of blazing star.

Native grassland plants hold their cards close to their stems, and closer to their roots. It's basic survival – don't waste resources, especially moisture. Most flower and set seed when spring snowmelt and rain have provided a surplus of moisture. From early moss phlox and prairie crocus to the later asters and blue grama grass, the show is short and quickly over. By late summer most have senesced, called it quits, gone to bed and retreated to their roots.

But not blazing star. It blooms late, providing a welcome splash of colour to a virtually universal hue of browns and yellows. While others wilt from the heat and dryness, it literally "blazes" in the dog days of late summer and into the autumn.

Blazing star is a forb in the aster family, and some of its relatives are late bloomers also. The plant has speckled leaves, earning it the Latin name of *Liatris punctata*, the latter word meaning dotted. So the common name is dotted blazing star.

Why it blooms late, outside of the period of better moisture, seems a mystery. Walt Whitman, in *Leaves of Grass*, touched on this when he wrote, "We feel the long pulsation, ebb and flow of endless motion / The tones of unseen mystery, the vague and vast suggestions." Maybe the plant has an inferiority complex, not wanting to compete with the subtle purple shades of the crocus, the wedding dress white of the saskatoon blossoms or the gaudy, highlighter yellow of the balsam root.

That it does bloom late is probably much appreciated by native bumblebees, butterflies and moths, since the lavender spike of flowers provides a late season buffet in lieu of the other prairie plants that have abandoned their pollinators.

Blazing star likely pulls few human heartstrings. Not only is it a prairie plant, living in a landscape that gets shunned by many, but it blooms past the time when the few native plant aficionados are keen to visit the flowers of the grassland.

Like most prairie plants, blazing star goes about its business quietly, largely out of sight and unheralded. However, early plant ecologists provide some insights on the plants of the native prairie environment, to which it would be worthwhile to pay attention.

Two of these, R.T. Coupland and R.E. Johnson from Saskatchewan, investigated how prairie plants make a living in dry conditions. Since moisture is the key to survival, they looked at root systems and rooting depths. They painstakingly excavated trenches in prairie soils and then disentangled the root systems of individual plants from the dirt. For anyone who has ever dug a hole by hand or tried to plant a fence post in these soils, the effort required for this work would have to be acknowledged as herculean.

For blazing star they found it drove its roots down to almost two metres into the soil. Another earlier researcher in Nebraska, John Weaver, found rooting depths for the plant to be nearly five metres! The rooting depth exceeds the above-ground portion of the plant by 13 to 33 times. Whitman was right on about "unseen mystery."

Compared to most other prairie plants, blazing star had deeper roots. This likely explains why it has the luxury of blooming late, when there is little or no surface moisture available. It taps deeper, subterranean sources of water. Like blazing star, though, none of the native grassland plants investigated had shallow roots (like introduced species do) and are admirably adapted to the semi-arid conditions of the prairies. To say these native plants are "drought-tolerant" seems like stereotypical understatement, obvious and trite.

Weaver was an early US prairie plant ecologist. In his 50-year career his investigations of the prairie were stellar and wide ranging. The bibliography of research papers he wrote or contributed to runs to four long pages. In one piece entitled "The Wonderful Prairie Sod," he said, "To the prairie sod only the plow is lethal."

In another paper Weaver pointed out, "Dotted blazing star develops slowly and is long lived. Ring counts in root crowns showed plant ages greater than 35 years." That requires a pause for reflection – 35 years! This is old-growth prairie, akin to old-growth forest.

On many levels, Weaver and others have consistently provided information on the elegant role, value and adaptability of prairie plants. There was a time this was not understood and, thinking grasslands could be "improved," we put much of that habitat under the plow. We are at a point now where it cannot be said we lack an understanding of the virtues and values of leaving these landscapes alone. Yet, even as we are better informed, we avoid using that information to make appropriate choices, and plow up more grassland.

Imagine what blazing star could teach us – if we had a mind to listen – about patience and persistence, of living successfully in a semi-arid environment, one undergoing the additional crisis of climate change. We prairie people could be similarly deeply rooted, parsimonious in water use and part of a community that thrives on natural diversity.

## STREAM TINKERING

----

I'm sure one of our Neanderthal ancestors looked around the family cave one day and thought, "This could stand a few improvements." From these humble beginnings we have evolved to be a species of tinkerers, constantly wanting to improve things, to upgrade, to remodel our surroundings.

It's one thing to design a better stone tool, like a spear point to skewer mammoths, to move from caves to castles and to transition from human power to atomic power. It's quite another to look at a landscape and say, "It's not good enough – I can make it better."

Our rivers and streams have become subject to this ancestral home improvement syndrome, especially with regard to fish habitat enhancement. I was subject to this hubris for a while myself. Attending fisheries conferences, seeing the images of trout stream improvements and hearing the glowing tales of more trout, and bigger ones too, made me a believer. Enthusiasm is a powerful motivator, but it needs to be tempered with reality.

My colleagues and I, in the now defunct Habitat Branch of the Fish and Wildlife Division, started tackling trout stream improvements, and also directing habitat restoration at things like pipeline crossings. These were all done in southwestern Alberta on trout streams in the foothills and mountains.

Improvements were designed to add pools, important to allow trout to overwinter better, to shore up eroding banks, creating overhead cover, and to add structural diversity to channels with little cover. We were working on the theory that if variety is the spice of life, adding more to streams would improve conditions for trout.

At the end of seven years of work, there were 351 habitat structures of four basic types on 26 streams. Then a team of fisheries biologists, a fluvial geomorphologist and a river hydraulics engineer began to evaluate whether these improvements had worked to increase habitat and trout. Evaluations were cursed (or blessed) with two flood events, and these revealed some striking outcomes.

Trying to anchor a structure in a stream subject to constant and sometimes dramatic shifts proved frustrating. Large boulders, meant to provide low-velocity resting areas, were subject to local scour and the boulders would disappear into the holes they had created. No matter how large the boulders – one was a Volkswagen-sized rock – they were swallowed. Some geologist in the far future may find one of these angular boulders emerging again from the substrate and ponder its origins.

In one case, rebuilding a stream bank obliterated by a pipeline crossing involved sinking rock anchors into large boulders, then sewing the boulders together in a conga line with thick cables. The result was a sinuous, stable stream bank with nooks and crannies where trout could find shelter. We thought we had also found the ticket to structure stability. Unfortunately, the stream had other plans and migrated to the other side of the valley. Some 40 years later it still hasn't seen fit to move back to use the bank we created for it.

The re-creation of overhanging stream banks, some damaged by livestock grazing, produced great shelter for trout in a small stream. After a minor flood event one structure was left solid and intact, but high and dry, as the stream had rafted the wood construction up onto the stream bank and then altered its course.

Rock and log weirs, built across the channel to encourage the stream to dig deep plunge pools, seemed successful but had inherent flaws. The plunge pools had a limited amount of low-velocity areas suitable as trout holding cover. An additional and crippling flaw was that as the depth of the pools increased with scour, this undermined the structures. As support was lost, they collapsed into the now deeper water. Bedload movement, the constant downstream flow of gravels and cobbles, then filled in the holes. Streams seemed intent on burying our attempts to improve things.

The short-term performance of these 351 instream structures, subject to a normal, small flood event, was encouraging, but not stellar. Nearly two-thirds survived and produced the designed habitat conditions. Then the flood of 1995 dampened our enthusiasm.

The results from post-flood evaluations sucked. The majority of structures had washed away, been buried or were severely damaged. Only a third still provided trout habitat. Streams with higher gradients and subject to flashier flow regimes downstream of mountain slopes had the highest structure failure rates.

This flood of 1995 was a big one, the one you expect to happen, on average, every century or so. Climate and land-use change show us that we can expect more of the same, with greater frequency and magnitude. This does not bode well for the longevity of instream habitat improvements.

Our efforts at habitat improvement were degraded by small flood events, and most did not survive a sizable flood. We had to reluctantly conclude these "improvements" were ephemeral and did not provide useful trout habitat over the long term. The term "ephemeral" is a good word to describe the fleeting, transitory and impermanent nature of such constructed habitats.

In our enthusiastic but ill-fated attempts to "train" streams to produce more trout habitat, they simply gave us the watery finger.

Not all habitat improvements were complete failures. Those that duplicated what nature had already provided seemed to work, like adding big logs and root wads to the stream. Log walls, to shore up eroding stream banks, endured when coupled with plantings of willow and aspen. Ironically, these structures were the cheapest to build and if washed away could be easily replaced.

We learned there are many flaws in the approach to stream habitat improvement. Trout populations are limited by a variety of factors, some involving physical habitats. Habitats created or improved should be ones that ease those habitat limitations, not just ones easy to construct. If these habitats are already present, maybe this is not what limits a population.

A shopping centre creates lots of space (habitat). If it only has one small hot dog vendor, there isn't enough food to support a lot of shoppers. Space is important, but food is essential. The limiting factor of stream productivity is overlooked in most habitat improvement projects. Stream productivity (aquatic and terrestrial insect production) will be a limiting factor beyond a certain trout population size; adding more habitat is like adding more vacant stores in the shopping mall.

When productivity is the limiting factor (and it is in cold, nutrient-poor Eastern Slopes streams), the end result is just moving the existing population around, like some kind of aquatic musical chairs. Studies confirm trout have more choice of habitats, but population size remains static.

Thinking we can fix or improve trout habitat is a bit like taking the back off a finely crafted Swiss watch, like a Rolex, and then poking the innards randomly with a large, flathead screwdriver in an effort to make it work better. This is tinkering gone feral, to indiscriminate fiddling. Compared to the watch, a stream is vastly more complicated. A watch keeps the time, but a stream has a pace, a rhythm, a makeup that would make a watchmaker pale in attempts to understand the complexity.

In a stream, pools occur with a size and frequency dependent on the waves of meander bends and the length between them. Each stream develops this cadence in balance with its own watershed. These relationships cannot be changed, and attempts to manipulate this, for example by attempting to increase the number of constructed pools, fail because streams won't let you bend the hydraulic and hydrologic rules.

It's easy to get sucked into a narrow focus for habitat improvement. If, in our perception, a stream wasn't built right from the beginning, without enough pools, overhanging banks or low velocity shelters, just add them. But if they don't persist there is no long-term benefit to the trout population.

A low-gradient stream in Wisconsin, or Ontario, and even a spring-fed brook like the North Raven River, might benefit from structural fixes. We shouldn't consider the techniques for improving the lot of trout in such streams as a template for our high-gradient Eastern Slopes ones. Under the thrall of improvement mania, it takes some time and failure to discern the differences.

One of the tests of being human is to be able to learn from mistakes. But some still haven't learned the lesson. To promote the eviscerating of mountains with coal mines, companies suggest that adding a few more pools to impacted streams should be adequate mitigation. Hack down the forest, and then mitigate that with a few Band-Aids on some eroding banks. Mitigation is one of those words, like radiation or poison, of which one should be wary.

In pondering the results of our foray into stream redesign, it is clear that constructed habitats failed to improve the lot of trout, especially the native species that are at risk in the Eastern Slopes. The things that worked were the things that were already part and parcel of a natural stream channel. Encouraging the restoration of riparian areas with revegetation, using bioengineering for eroding banks and for dealing with soil compaction from random camping and off-highway vehicle use provide simpler, more effective and long-lived options. Riparian restoration also deals with other essentials, like stream shading, nutrient additions and providing the building blocks of physical trout habitat.

This is why logging riparian areas, and providing ridiculously narrow buffers, is such a monumentally bad land-use decision. Streams need wood to build habitat for trout. Log jams create overhead cover and deep pools. Logs that stretch across channels moderate stream gradients, in a stair-stepped fashion, building low-velocity areas key to juvenile trout survival. Logs, with their root wads intact, pivot parallel to the flow, offering bank protection and overhead trout cover. Riparian areas supply that wood. Natural instream structures are impermanent, but as long as riparian areas remain a source for large wood, a dynamic equilibrium is met.

In thinking more broadly, the best, most effective way to improve the situation for trout requires us to look after the watershed, not just the channel in which they swim. Even the best riparian management cannot deal with excessive sediment and a shift in hydrologic response that brings both floods and drought, sometimes in the same season.

Our spatial and road footprint is large and grows larger in trout territory. The number of culverts that impede trout passage are legion. Evidence mounts that wicked weather on top of an excessive land-use footprint will increase the frequency, magnitude and duration of flooding. This destabilizes stream channels and trout habitat.

Trying to fix our upstream land-use excesses in downstream portions of a watershed is fighting gravity. It is futile. Like throwing rocks and sticks into the stream.

## WILDLIFE WE LOVE TO HATE

As some wild creatures adapt to us and our ways – like raccoons, skunks, mice, magpies, gulls, coyotes and sparrows – we are exasperated by this close association. In a similar strategy to weeds, some wildlife species thrive in human-disturbed landscapes. But instead of watching with interest and enjoyment this evolutionary magic at work, we rail against these wild creatures that frustrate us.

We do try to make distinctions about origins. Some of the wildlife that plague us are, indeed, native. They belong here and their ancestors were likely frequenting the habitats that became our backyards. Others are imports, like English sparrows, starlings, Eurasian collared doves and domestic pigeons. I suppose that gives us some room for wildlife bigotry, except someone brought them here, they prospered, and the genie is long out of the bottle.

They eat our garbage (which we are throwing out anyway); occasionally they eat our cats (which seems poetic justice for the millions of wild birds eaten by cats every year); consume our shrubbery (which we planted to replace the native vegetation); collide with our cars (because we are willfully blind to their travels and routes); wake us up too early with their raucous calls (which ignores the noise of our human lives); and crap indiscriminately on our cars, decks and shoulders from their aerial perches (which seems only fitting, given the circumstances).

In my case our urban home is shaded by old, sweeping elm trees that are non-native. One is the favoured perch for a merlin, a small falcon that likes to pluck its victims (usually English sparrows) from one branch. The elm tree is affected by a scale insect that produces honeydew, which filters down, coating my truck with the sticky substance. As the feathers float down, they adhere to the sap on the truck, giving it the appearance of having been tarred and feathered. It makes for mixed feelings about wildlife, even on my part.

The merlins have made Christians out of the English sparrows. They now believe in and fear a supreme being. Skittish, far from bold, the sparrows now cower in the shrubbery. No longer do they hog the neighbour's bird bath, only dashing in for a quick splash, apprehensively looking over their shoulders as they do.

My perception is that the sparrow numbers are down and the native birds, the nuthatches, chickadees and juncos, are prospering in the sparrow void. Perhaps the native birds are much more in tune with the merlins, having evolved together for millennia, and are less susceptible to predation.

Even in an urban neighbourhood where things are turned topsy-turvy with our interventions, some aspect of balance, of a dynamic equilibrium, sorts itself out. A truck covered in feathers is a small price to pay for more native birds, less bird droppings on the backyard picnic table and a gang of sparrows dispersed, displaced and maybe digested.

Our neighbourhood has become home range to a small herd of mule deer. We like to refer to them as our living lawn ornaments. They, like other critters, provide a tangible reminder of wild things in a very urban setting. But their presence provokes a mixed response. They browse on the shrubbery, part of landscaped lawns. Some neighbours have resorted to fencing to dissuade this plunder of ornamental shrubs. One neighbour has had a negative interaction between a doe and her dog – fortunately with no ill effects on either side. Another neighbour feeds the herd apple slices. It's evident there is no consensus on how the mule deer are viewed – somewhere between grudging sufferance grading to wonder.

We will tolerate these apparent trespassers, interlopers and vagabonds until their ability to adapt to us seems too clever and we think they have crossed some artificial boundary of privilege. As if we have some divine right to use all of the space and resources the world holds! At what point is it "our" world and not theirs? When does it become "their" world, and then do we need permission to enter?

Basically, what galls us is that these wild creatures show no respect for us and our property. Of course, we don't act in a reciprocal fashion, respecting the need of wild creatures to feed themselves, find appropriate habitats and reproduce, with the same zeal we approach these necessary ecological requirements for ourselves. How do you spell "presumptuous"? If we can't revise our attitudes and behaviours towards these species who trespass onto "our" land, we are probably incapable of understanding our role in any part of the natural world.

Anything wild that can manage to thrive in the pacified, manufactured and domesticated landscapes of our making should not just be tolerated but honoured, cherished and maybe even supported. You'd think we could manage to share a little space with the original residents and some immigrants.

For many people, these vexing creatures are the only association with anything remotely wild they will encounter in their lives. If some of these creatures create some connections in people's minds with the wider, wilder world, that's not a bad thing. Wildlife and their habitats need all the support that can be mustered.

I guess we humans are happy to embrace nature as long as nature doesn't tread on our toes, move into our neighbourhoods, eat our food and mess up our lives.

As long as nature isn't too natural, we can tolerate it.

## SMOKING HOLY GRASS

No, not *that* grass! I'm referring to sweetgrass, a grass that seems to bridge the gap between the plant kingdom and the animal one, where humans reside. We eat plant material, cure ourselves with it, occasionally harm ourselves, gape at the beauty and intricacy, but sweetgrass does one better. It can be ceremonial, medicinal, hygienic, utilitarian and inspirational.

Sweetgrass used to have the Latin name of *Hierochloë odorata*, literally "fragrant holy grass." Plant taxonomists continually tinker with species placement and names, and now its official scientific name is *Anthoxanthum hirtum*. Whatever the name, Shakespeare would say, it "would smell as sweet."

Diving in, nose first, some say sweetgrass is redolent with tones of vanilla. This fragrance is produced by a compound called coumarin, an aromatic, organic chemical. Its role might be to produce a chemical defence against predators of the plant, but the science explanation has a way of taking away some of the mystery and romance.

My nose isn't as discriminating, and when I smell the flat, bright and shiny green leaves my reaction is different. Sweetgrass likes to keep its feet wet, in riparian settings like stream sides, wetland margins and swales where runoff periodically collects. To me the plant evokes a sense of clean, earthy outdoors – an intact, healthy place and one so nice you just feel like rolling in it.

We grow a patch of sweetgrass in our backyard. It has an exuberant growth and seems to thrive, spreading ever outward. The patch is not yet big enough for us to roll in, but it has become the go-to grass for our dog to graze. We don't know if it's the taste, the medicinal effect or its effect as a breath sweetener. The jury is still out on the latter attribute.

Our harvest is respectful; as Robin Wall Kimmerer in *Braiding Sweetgrass* points out, the plant thrives under a light cutting. A modest pile of leaves, each up to 40 centimetres long, accumulates and the odour wafts over us. As Kimmerer writes, "Breathe it in and you start to remember things you didn't know you'd forgotten."

For me it's the pang of a memory from a wetland on the farm I was raised on. I wouldn't have been able to identify sweetgrass then – it would have been just part of the greenery of the pasture. As the molecules of scent circulated in my nose from the cut leaves of our backyard patch, I recognized that odour and was transported back in time to the edge of that puddle of a wetland.

Braiding sweetgrass, we follow the tradition of dividing the leaves into three sections, representing mind, body and soul. Each section has seven leaves in it, for the seven generations before us, the seven teachings (love, respect, honesty, courage, wisdom, truth and humility) and the seven generations in front of us. Sections are then interlaced together forming a flat, solid, three-stranded structure. The act of braiding is like entwining ourselves with the plant.

Sweetgrass braids do not burst into flame when lit but rather smoulder away, releasing a plume of thin smoke, like that of a Cuban cigar. Unlike the harshness of the cigar smoke, burning sweetgrass is more like the gentle scent of a sachet of potpourri. Instead of choking you or making your eyes water, the mildly pungent smoke envelops you and has a calming effect.

When my wife burns sweetgrass for her regular yoga sessions, the aura of it permeates the house, not setting off the smoke alarms but creating a meditative effect. It is evident why Indigenous Peoples have long used sweetgrass for prayer, smudging and purifying. The plant is a gift. In its giving, sweetgrass has the potential, if we let it, to transport us to a place of mindfulness, positive energy and connectivity with the Earth.

All of us engage in some type of ceremony in our lives, from the morning ritual of waiting for the coffee to percolate to customary greetings with friends and colleagues and, for some, the pageantry of religion. I've become quite taken with a simpler ceremony, one where a plant can remind us the ground we walk on is special, even sacred and worth stewarding.

## A SMALL BUNDLE OF LARGE ENTHUSIASMS
### *The Underappreciated Chickadee*

In a popularity contest you might think a cute, chatty, friendly and gregarious contestant would be the hands-down winner. That was not the case when Alberta chose its provincial bird, the great horned owl, in a province-wide children's vote. Now, I have nothing against the stately, nocturnal owl and the symbolism over threatened wildlife. I just find the attribute most commonly linked to owls – wisdom – isn't always evident in Alberta. Some behaviours of provincial politicians and parties might have had people selecting the seagull as the representative bird. It squawks incessantly, squabbles with everyone and shits over everything. But I digress.

As I walked to work one morning, in the midst of a polar vortex of sub-zero temperatures and ice fog, I wondered if I had engaged in a fool's errand, even as well dressed as I was. Snow squeaking under my feet was the only sound, until I came near a bit of low shrubbery next to a tall spruce tree. Then there was that unmistakable call, *chick-a-dee-dee-dee*. A flock of small birds with black caps and bibs busily investigated the nooks and crannies of several trees and shrubs.

These chickadees buoyed my spirits on my frosty trudge. Any creature that small, surviving and thriving in an Alberta winter, certainly would have had my vote for our provincial bird. With a matchbox-sized body and a furnace the size of your little fingernail, one can only shiver in amazement at a chickadee's ability to tolerate freezing temperatures. Observing them roosting in our juniper tree at −30°C, all puffed up in their own down jackets, was a study in thermodynamics.

Most interactions with the bird are in urban environments, but the chickadee is no city wimp. Evolution has crafted a bird superbly able to weather our climate. Aldo Leopold whimsically observed that evolution had shrunk the chickadee "until he was just too big to be snapped up by flycatchers as an insect, and just too little to be pursued by hawks and owls as meat." Their small size does ratchet up the challenges of survival, though, as Leopold alluded to with, "It seems likely that weather is the only killer so devoid of both humour and dimension as to kill a chickadee."

For most wildlife, surviving through the winter is a test. In the case of chickadees they must eat the equivalent of a third of their body weight during the day to survive a winter's night. They also have the ability to reduce their body temperature to conserve energy, in what is termed nocturnal hypothermia. Shivering is another mechanism to adapt to bone-chilling cold. That, and having a fluffy coat of down that weighs 10 per cent of the bird, is complemented by finding good roost sites that keep them out of the wind. Even so, overnight a bird can lose most of the weight accumulated through the day.

Although it wouldn't be popular, going into partial hypothermia and shivering overnight might be the ultimate weight loss technique for us overfed humans. Theoretically, the human equivalent would be a 90-kilogram individual shivering through a cold night and emerging (hopefully) in the morning nine kilograms lighter.

Dr. Andrew Hurly, of the University of Lethbridge, identified one possible complication of bulking up too much in an investigation of winter energy budgeting of chickadees. If you're too fat, you lose manoeuvrability and speed, putting yourself at risk of predation. But not enough fat reserves and you may not wake up the next morning. It's a delicate dance these birds do. Maybe there's another message for humans in terms of overconsumptive habits – take only what you need.

With a small body and a smaller heating plant, these birds are constant foragers during the day. Sometimes a feeding frenzy signals a significant weather change. Like Grandpa John with his arthritic knee, chickadees can sense barometric pressure changes warning them of an oncoming blizzard. That frenzy to forage is to stock up on body fat and also to cache food for a prolonged stay during inclement conditions.

They seem to have an innate investigative ability, honed in the crucible of time, to discern food sources. In the fall, when house flies and other insects seek refuge in the cracks between the siding of our cabin, chickadees have a picnic. We are ignored, as is our gift of peanuts, as the flock swoops, strafes and skewers one fly after another. It's not for us to dictate taste.

Perched high up in a tree stand one cold day, I watched a flock of chickadees working the aspen forest for food. Although the meaning of the calls was lost on me, it was a pleasant bit of chattering. One bird made a beeline towards me, swooping in under my parka. I think it mistook me for an appendage to the tree, a large piece of bark that had sloughed off the trunk and sheltered many insect eggs. I felt it investigating, with tiny claws digging into my underlayer. Perhaps it was perplexed as to why it was so warm under the hunk of bark and yet there were no insects to harvest. I sensed its disappointment with me as a food source as it flew off with its flock.

The call the bird made after emerging, empty-beaked, from beneath my parka may have been a chickadee curse. Researchers have identified that chickadee flocks have as many as 14 calls with specific meanings. These may contain some of the characteristics of human language. These are talkative birds, constantly in communication, with high, wheezy notes, in addition to the trademark call that names the bird.

When I hear that cheerful song of *chick-a-dee-dee-dee*, it transcends writings, speeches and art to connect with one of Earth's creatures.

I understand chickadees are engaged in the endless pursuit of survival and everything they do is linked to that prime directive. And yet, observing an active flock, acrobatic in their flight, curious to the point of tameness and vocal in an obvious social context makes one think of joy and the exuberance of life. These little birds never fail to inspire me (and maybe you) to see beyond the trials and travails of life to the gift of simple pleasures.

In the chickadee we have an underappreciated bird, part of a suite of biodiversity treasures to which we pay scant attention. In an apt description, Leopold said the chickadee was a small bundle of large enthusiasms. I would agree! This bird is unassuming, harmless, on the edge of our consciousness, yet has much to teach us hulking, greedy humans about survival, restraint and maybe joy.

*Illustration by Liz Saunders*

# 7

# The Naked Biologist

*Listen, and you will realize that we are*
*made not from cells or from atoms.*
*We are made from stories.*

—Mia Couto

## REVELATIONS ON COMBAT BIOLOGY

———

Elevated like the vertebrae of a whale beached on land, a series of north-south trending ridges lie just outside the Livingstone Range in southwestern Alberta. Twisted limber pine on the ridge tops, enormous Douglas firs on the slopes and a covering of rough fescue grasslands provide a sylvan scene of wild country. Only the occasional fence and truck trail detract from the sense of untrammelled wilderness. This is the Whaleback.

It was nearly not so. Beneath the shag rug of fescue grasslands and elk winter range lie pockets of natural gas – sour, hydrogen-sulfide-rich gas. This attracted Amoco, an international petroleum giant (formerly the Standard Oil Company built by John D. Rockefeller).

It appeared Amoco thought, with their deep connections to the Alberta government, they could skate through the regulatory hurdles with a minimum amount of public and community involvement. It was evident both Amoco and the Alberta government wanted to avoid a regulatory hearing and proceed with development of the gas field under "standard" (read minimal) operating conditions. Any thought of an environmental impact assessment (EIA) was squashed at senior levels within the government department ostensibly charged with protecting fish and wildlife, even though the site contained critical elk winter range, then the second largest in Alberta.

Biologists (including me) working within the Fish and Wildlife Division were stymied. Though we remained concerned about the implications of industrial development in the region, we were not permitted to discuss the utility of an EIA with Amoco, or anyone outside the department. However, there was a chink in the gag-order armour. The Energy Resources Conservation Board (ERCB), which was the regulatory body of the day, was obligated to make public any correspondence about a proposed gas field development.

Fish and Wildlife biologists reached out to a like-minded individual within the ERCB and had him make a verbal request (nudge, nudge, wink, wink) to the Fish and Wildlife Division about what would be needed to assess the environmental impacts of the proposed development. They responded with a letter to the ERCB on all the necessary components of an impact assessment that would address issues and concerns related to fish and wildlife populations and their habitats. Since the letter was transmitted within government and followed standard protocols no one broke any rules.

When the terms and conditions of a possible EIA related to fish and wildlife issues became public through the exchange of letters with the ERCB, it threw a wrench into the tightly scripted and controlled agenda to slide a potentially harmful development past the noses of Albertans. An ERCB hearing was eventually held, and the rest is history.

It became apparent Amoco had not done their homework on assessing environmental impacts, had grossly underestimated the impact on wildlife and the local human community, and could not persuade the Board they could safely extract high-risk gas from the field.

In an almost precedent-setting decision for a petroleum-dominated province, the ERCB concluded that the project was not in the public interest, effectively telling Amoco to go away. The Nature Conservancy of Canada became involved and raised enough funding to buy back the mineral rights from Amoco. This sparked protected area status for the Whaleback, perhaps forever ending the risk from industrial development.

If this small group of concerned biologists had merely stood by, had strictly followed orders to remain quiet and let events unfold, it is likely the Whaleback now would be an industrial site with multiple roads, wellsites, compressor stations, pipelines, the rotten-egg stench of sour gas emissions, constant truck traffic, power lines, weeds, sediment – and no elk. This is the essence of combat biology.

Combat biology is a term introduced by Holly Doremus and Dan Tarlock in their book *Water War in the Klamath Basin: Macho Law, Combat Biology, and Dirty Politics*. This form of combat involves words and ideas rather than bayonets and bombs, yet the metaphor aptly captures the essence of the process.

Describing combat biology in war terms may seem dramatic, but not all wars are military – although, at times, the metaphor can seem frighteningly similar, since many biologists often work under fire.

The concept of combat biology isn't well understood, even by many biologists. A researcher, looking into the hidden life of a creature, defining essential habitat or diet, or using DNA to identify new species, isn't likely to be a combat biologist. An academic, teaching the fundamentals of ecology to young, compliant and willing minds may not encounter the phenomenon. A consulting biologist, defining impacts for a proposed project and recommending mitigative solutions, may dance on the edge of combat biology, but not be completely immersed.

This field is largely restricted to those biologists who operate at the interface of resource use and protection, who have seen the impacts of resource exploitation and who can predict the ecological outcomes of proposed development schemes. They bear the scar tissue created from seeing landscapes fragmented, ecological thresholds surpassed, and populations diminish and sometimes wink out even though all the land-use conditions, guidelines, policies and mitigative strategies were followed. These are the people who stand in the way of the "just git 'er dun" mentality – the argot of industry, motorized recreation and the short-term mentality evidenced in the rush to turn natural resources and wild areas into stock dividends and muddy ruts.

Biologists who hold up their hands, physically and metaphorically, to say, "This is too much, you are leaving too little; this is irreplaceable"; and "All the king's horses and all the king's men will not be able to reassemble this marvellously, interconnected, intertangled work of natural art," understand, implicitly, combat biology. They ask the difficult, the penetrating and the embarrassing questions. To the chagrin of politicians, industry and organizations blind to consequences, they point out the inconsistencies, the errors and the lies in the dreams and schemes of resource exploitation.

Combat biology does not involve environmental activism, although some, in sheer frustration, are drawn to it. It is advocacy, though, giving voice to concerns about the future well-being of fish, wildlife and plant populations, the essential habitats they rely on, and the space required for them to survive and thrive.

There might be a tendency to view combat biology and those who practise it as underhanded, sneaky and unethical. Some equate it with being science-lite, or science-select, twisting facts to support a preconceived outcome.

I take an alternate view. Although any technique can be abused, combat biology, as I have seen it used, involves the application of science to find solutions to problems and the use of reliable, factual evidence to guide decisions. Often, it is a process of postulating effects, then testing the assumptions to predict outcomes and minimize management uncertainties.

At its essence, the art of combat biology is understanding the levers to pull or push, knowing who controls those levers and encouraging those responsible for the levers to move the system in a way that benefits ecological health, resilience and the persistence of wild creatures.

Combat biology applies a combination of data, research, experience, communication skills and strategic thinking to help the public, politicians and industry understand impacts and consequences. It is often a message not only scorned, but unwanted. Most combat biologists are not dissuaded by this and employ other methods to plant ideas. On reflection, many biologists in this role would say they might have been better served with backgrounds in psychology or sociology than with academic training in biology.

This follows a basic understanding that science cannot give us all the answers. Combat biologists recognize the fact that the most difficult questions and the most persistent problems are not matters of science, but of values. Science may tell us what is happening and can help us understand the consequences of various choices, but it can't make us do anything about it or tell us which choices to make.

Although it is tempting to unleash the artillery of facts, to blast by broadside a barrage of data, changing minds is a more nuanced affair. Facts, evidence and the weight of science often aren't enough. Conflicts boil down to disagreements over values and priorities, even though they often masquerade as arguments over data. Even if the evidence is perfect, decisions can't be reduced to an algorithm.

So a combat biologist attempts to illuminate the problem in ways to indicate options, choices and consequences. Any communication effort integrates three components: the message, the messaging and the messenger. Imagery, humour and stories are used as vital pieces of effective communication. Sometimes the source of the message (often a combat biologist) is seen to lack credibility and the message is unheeded. Shrewd biologists employ, through collaborative efforts with other like-minded individuals and organizations, arm's length mechanisms to get messages out, to exert pressure and to ask the difficult questions.

In the arsenal of a combat biologist are techniques to evoke nostalgia, empathy, guilt and stewardship. These are combined with pragmatic devices like avoiding prosecution, saving money, understanding cumulative effects and maintaining social licence.

Classic in simplicity, and a teachable moment in its use, is the explanation of shifting baselines, helping people see that the decisions of the past (and today) remove options for the future. It can be an effective counterweight to the notion that our resource-use footprint isn't cumulative in both space and time. Today is a shadow of yesterday – it is a mere slice, and the more slices we carve with our resource-use decisions the poorer we become in fish and wildlife, wild places and options.

Biologists are not mindless automatons, responding only to the direction of bureaucrats, politicians and corporate voices. We are not "captured" by the organizations that employ us, or the industries and activities we help regulate. Our profession is one of caring about and for wild things, nature and the web of life that we all require to survive. To suggest biologists should subvert those principles for the sake of political ideology, economics or the latest fad, fashion and craze is untenable.

There was a time (and it may still be with us) when saying "no" to a development proposal was tantamount to career suicide. This was the Alberta Advantage, interpreted by some to mean no development proposal could be rejected. In response, some of my inventive colleagues learned how to tailor a "no" in a way that sounded like a "yes." This was accomplished by ensuring the conditions for approval were onerous and crafted to achieve a conservation objective.

Sometimes the combination of pre-development inventories, cumulative effects assessments, buffer zones, project redesign, access controls, noise abatement, timing constraints and extensive monitoring requirements coupled with mitigation to fully restore fish and wildlife habitats to pre-development conditions proved too expensive, time consuming and logistically difficult. This provided the proponent the opportunity to consider whether the development was worth it. Some decided it wasn't.

Combat biologists understand the rules, but they have not drunk the corporate Kool-Aid. As the saying goes, "Others make the rules, we play the game." If one understands the rules one can anticipate where the flexibility might exist and how to stretch the envelope to achieve a better ecological outcome. This follows an (unwritten) axiom of bureaucracy: "Rules are for the guidance of the wise and the rigid adherence to by fools." Rules only provide a rough approximation of the boundaries; aspects of vision, principles and strategy are more important determinants of a combat biologist's motivation.

Some might find the attitude to rules and their evasion troubling. Combat biologists don't. As a rule, they operate on two principles: "If you have to ask, the answer is no," and, "It is better to beg for forgiveness, than sometimes to ask permission."

A challenge that combat biologists must grapple with, especially those in government service, is that the stated objectives of an organization may not square with how an organization operates. If an organization hires competent professionals to do the job of managing, conserving or protecting biodiversity values, it makes little sense to ignore their advice, to fail to seek their advice or to stifle the provision of advice.

This is an institutional failure where the perversity of organizing a thing (like biodiversity conservation) is that soon there is an inclination to pay more attention to the needs of the organization than the values for which the organization was originally organized. Combat biologists rarely forget the prime directive of their task. Combat biologists go about their tasks quietly, for to shine too much light on their activities is as detrimental to them as it might be to a shy, retiring wild creature. But they understand, cerebrally as well as viscerally, that evolution gave us a neck and meant us to stick it out. Combat biology is about finding solutions and effective strategies rather than accepting inertia. In contrast, playing it safe, not rocking the boat and being risk-averse is not an inspirational philosophy for ethical behaviour, nor is the ecological outcome helpful.

There is no organization of combat biologists, although they know well among themselves who they are. If they were to rally behind a slogan, it might well be "Whatever works!"

## FEAR AND INTIMIDATION IN ALBERTA RESOURCE MANAGEMENT

"Bullying: when you stand up to it, it stops." This message is broadcast regularly in the media by the Government of Alberta. Advice is more credible if it comes from a source that walks the talk.

John Taggart's brown hair is now grizzled, like some of the bears he used to capture in his early career with Alberta Fish and Wildlife. A touch of grey in the hair colouring doesn't signal a change, or any compromise from the black-and-white attitude John has held towards fish and wildlife habitat, especially its protection in the face of myriad land uses.

Now retired, he is beyond the bullying and intimidation used on such unbending, unrepentant defenders of wildlife in government service. John tranquilized many animals over the years. Subsequently, senior government bureaucrats, politicians and industry captains probably secretly dreamt of sedating him over his stance on protecting wildlife.

In appearance John seems to be an unlikely cross between Elvis and a Mafia don, maybe Genghis Khan. In both of the latter cases, one you would wish to be on your side for his fierce defence of fish and wildlife. A poor choice for the diplomatic dance of negotiation, he often framed his concerns and comments in small words and short sentences. John never suffered social desirability bias, a fancy term for telling people what they want to hear. In short, John was a poor person to select to put pressure on to change his recommendations on habitat issues.

If only John could have continued working with bears and other "problem" wildlife. He would never have been exposed to the controversial, gut-wrenching pursuit of habitat protection, in its own way perhaps more dangerous than wrestling bears. In a province that touts itself as "open for business," the philosophy of the Alberta Advantage is anything but sympathetic to environmental interests like protecting biodiversity.

Many of Alberta's public who cherish a healthy, natural world probably suffer from the perfectly reasonable delusion that people like John are tasked by government to protect fish and wildlife, to ensure biodiversity persists. Others, closer to the action, observe that when government thinks of biologists, which isn't often, it doesn't think much of them because of the perceived impediments to economic development of their recommendations.

To understand this loathing for biologists one can turn to lawyers. Perhaps the start of lawyer jokes and the unfair rap laid on the profession starts with Dick the Butcher, a character in Shakespeare's *Henry VI*. The line that is so controversial and provocative is Dick saying: "The first thing we do, let's kill all the lawyers." Contrary to popular understanding this was not intended to be anti-lawyer or to serve as the basis for future criticism of the profession. Rather, the phrase relates to singling out and eliminating those who might stand in the way of a contemplated revolution, the truth tellers, and defenders of civil society.

In a parallel fashion, we could apply this to biologists as well, especially government ones. Dick's argument is just as relevant to this profession, especially with the real-life propensity to silence, censure or fire biologists who might criticize development or policy and stand in the way of economic progress. At least the conventional wisdom in moneyed and policy circles is that biologists impede the necessary wheels of progress.

Perhaps it is because biologists try to take the larger, long-term view of the situation, and aren't as mesmerized, as their critics seem to be, by short-term profits underwritten by foregoing future options and externalizing expenses to society and the environment.

There's nothing built into the laws of nature or the artifices of politics that says biologists have to be listened to – but if they are not, the consequences can be grave. Sadly, the Alberta government often sees the role of its biologists not so much to advise on ecological issues in resource developments as to rubber-stamp approvals and to be the unfortunate buffer between bad decisions and adverse public opinion. John either never got the stamp or steadfastly refused to use it.

John began his career in habitat protection as part of the Habitat Branch, a now defunct part of the Fish and Wildlife Division. His "territory" was northwestern Alberta, where he managed, with his unyielding, uncompromising ways, to anger both the timber industry and the captains of oil and gas. One might argue that some strategic compromises, some softening of approach, might have yielded different results, but that was not John's style. In his words, "They [industry and the Forest Service] have their job and I have mine." One has to admire the singularity of purpose.

Following the demise of the Habitat Branch – a politically motivated hatchet job with the acquiescence of senior bureaucrats – John was summarily transferred to Medicine Hat. Medicine Hat, in the grasslands of Alberta, was thought to be far enough from a forested landscape that John could cause industry no more trouble. In an ironic twist, the first referral John dealt with in his new posting was one of timber harvest in the Cypress Hills.

In a spiral of ironies, sending John to the grasslands to handle habitat protection seems, in retrospect, one of the dumber moves of government bureaucracy. Alberta's grasslands, since provincehood, have shrunk substantially more than any other natural region. Not surprisingly, this is a landscape more at risk, with more species imperilled, than collectively anywhere else in Alberta. To conservation-minded individuals, who saw a need for a high level of habitat protection to ensure grassland species and their habitats didn't wink out under unremitting resource pressure, John's principled approach was appreciated, mostly silently.

It's an understatement to say a tension zone existed between economic and environmental interests before John arrived, and subsequent events exacerbated the issues. Adding John to the mix only piled fuel on an incipient blaze.

The fuse was lit, and although it burned a long time, finally the powder was reached. A seemingly innocuous referral dealing with wind energy development created the ensuing explosion. The reaction, especially of bureaucrats, spoke volumes about the incestuous relationship between political and corporate worlds.

Like the plot in a detective novel, the path of this drama is about the money. Dangling in the breeze, just out of reach of the wind farm developer, was a federal government subsidy worth millions of dollars. As a national objective the subsidy was designed to kick-start and level the field for green energy development, making it more palatable for investors, to help with the process of weaning us from non-renewable energy sources. However laudatory the goal, when green energy like wind development meets the ground the results are not always so environmentally friendly.

A developer, spurred by thoughts of federal government largesse, eyed a substantial piece of seemingly vacant grassland for wind turbine installation. Wind-powered electrical generation may seem green, but the footprint of development can be just as invasive as that of its carbon-emitting cousin – the petroleum industry.

John, in his usual forthright way, pointed out the inconsistency of this "green" initiative, with its potential impact on native grasslands and the increasing suite of imperilled species. As such, he provided his recommendations to the developer (and copied the regulator, the Alberta Utilities Commission) that the project was not in the best interests of ecosystem integrity or of wildlife.

That's when the powder ignited. Without Fish and Wildlife approval, a sign-off over concerns, the tap for the millions in federal subsidies would remain closed. One can only surmise the chain of events, from a developer cut off from federal tax dollars to the calls to local politicians and cabinet members about the "over-zealous" response blocking development. In due course John was asked to change his recommendations, to allow the development to proceed. Given John's history, his answer was predictable.

What followed can be characterized as pure theatre, although not very entertaining from John's perspective. A conciliatory attempt was made to convince John to show more "flexibility" – to consider adaptive management and mitigation. No greenhorn, John knew these were empty, virtually meaningless terms, designed as a means to an industry end and not to protect prairie.

The screws tightened with veiled threats about implications of his intransigence to the provincial Wildlife program, for future budgets and staff positions. But John remained firm: "This is my recommendation – if you don't like it, make your own changes." What John understood, implicitly, was that he was not going to be the fall guy, the sacrificial biologist, if the deal went bad and bureaucrats and politicians needed someone to shoulder the blame.

A biologist provides a recommendation, a professional opinion, based on several lines of evidence, relevant policies and experience. That recommendation is not a decision – it is advice. The province hires professionals, ostensibly to convey that advice to decision makers. If the advice is not accepted, especially if it runs counter to some corporate or political agenda, it is not an option, nor is it acceptable to exert pressure on a professional to change their advice.

The responsibility to accept, ignore or change the recommendation must come from senior bureaucrats, and inevitably the political level. It is also the level where accountability for any decision lies. The repercussions of a bad decision, adverse public reaction or even legal challenges do not follow the chain down to the resource professional.

It's clear the bureaucrats involved either were ignorant of this fundamental separation or chose to ignore it. Blunt orders – "you will sign off" – followed. But what departmental officials hadn't reckoned on was that when increasing force is applied to an immovable object like John, no movement occurs. Apparently, none of them had either listened to or understood the 1960s Simon and Garfunkel tune "I Am a Rock."

After three separate refusals to sign off on the wind farm development, John was put through a disciplinary process and given a letter of reprimand for failing to comply with a direct order. It clearly sounds like they confused John with someone in uniform rather than a resource professional. This punitive and, to a major degree, petty reaction to "insubordination" persisted even after a low-level management official tucked his ethics away and signed off on the insult to native grassland.

One might have thought the pressure on John to "sign off" was in the same league as having Galileo recant the heresy that the Earth revolves around the sun. Of course, in Alberta, where everything revolves around money, the draconian response to John's habitat protection recommendations isn't surprising. But when superiors put substantial pressure on subordinate professionals to meet certain political or corporate expectations, especially to give the political bosses the protection of plausible deniability, it is a dynamic where the public interest is subverted in a sinister way.

John had faced more ferocious adversaries – a grizzly in Banff that had mauled several people resulting in the death of one – but in such situations he was well armed. A fish and wildlife habitat biologist has few armaments. Other than knowledge, intuition and experience, there's not much else. The information on habitat requirements, population status, critical habitat locations and status, plus cumulative effects analysis to allow a sense of what one more development means, is rarely complete, adequate or sometimes even present to support a recommendation.

Arrayed against the biologist is a formidable economic juggernaut with strong political connections. There is little patience for exhaustive reviews (the turnaround time for referrals is counted in days), little patience for delays and little evidence of the stewardship ethic touted in corporate vision statements.

In the broadest sense, our biological professionals are caretakers of some special public resources. There is an expectation that the resources entrusted to their care will be managed well and passed on undiminished. It's hard to do that in today's Alberta. The dogma of doing everything, everywhere, anytime and all the time runs counter to their sense of responsibility, and that creates angst. As caretakers they must feel they have no voice, no clout or recourse and will be held accountable even under circumstances beyond their control.

Support mechanisms are few, and the general public, who apparently, from numerous surveys, want protection of fish and wildlife, are too disconnected to see what biologists do on their behalf and the hurdles these professionals face. One might think support should be present internally, but in John's case, which mirrors others in Alberta's civil service, the reaction was punitive.

As a general rule these situations never become public, so we never see the machinations of politicians and bureaucrats. Coercion of the civil service is corrosive, and it is shielded from public view by the mazes and fences of bureaucracy, a labyrinth too impenetrable for the average citizen.

The veiled message to staff is clear: take an obedient place in the department and become a compliant cog in the wheels of economic progress. Let the wheels spin and don't look or think critically about the impacts. Fears of discipline, demotion, relocation or dismissal are powerful tools to maintain the message. This atmosphere of acquiescence masquerades under the contrived guise of teamwork.

Professionals the government employs are pressured to act unprofessionally when the government wants a different answer. I'm not sure we can ask less of professionals than to act professionally – bounded by ethics, a code of conduct, using good science and not acquiescing to the corporate mantra. I'd say we could (and should) ask the same of bureaucrats and politicians.

One of the true measures of being a resource professional is not engaging in clairvoyant behaviour – anticipating what a client, a supervisor or a politician wants to hear, instead of what they need to hear. Anything else is resource "pillow talk," a position held too close to provide objective, factual, rational, truthful recommendations.

The place called Alberta is busy with drilling, plowing, cutting, building, digging, dumping and diverting. It wouldn't be surprising that this creates an unremitting and thankless workload for biologists in assessing implications for habitat and biodiversity. Equally unsurprising is that the recommendations made on at least some of this economic activity are going to make someone mad.

It is evident government (and industry) does not like to hear what it needs to – rather it limits itself to what it wants to hear. If government doesn't like the message, the recommendations and the advice, wouldn't it be simpler to avoid all the trouble and go straight to the answer of *yes* to development?

The problem is, even the political and corporate worlds need credibility in things environmental. Both need the impression that decisions, often bad ones about environmental issues, are being made at arm's length, ostensibly by objective professionals.

It is so much better public relations if there is an aura of responsibility and concern for the environment, and the impression of critically balancing protection against economic development. To accomplish this requires the construction of a veneer of scientific backing for what is an ideological response.

When the Alberta government speaks of balance – the delicate adjustment between environmental protection and economic development – I think of the pressure placed on wildlife professionals to acquiesce to development. It puts one in mind of the shifty storekeeper with one concealed thumb on the scale, in his favour. But to ask the hired help to engage in this deception is unconscionable. To badger, threaten and coerce provincial employees into changing recommendations against their professional judgment is deceitful and unethical.

This incident came at the end of John's public service career. Knowing the punishment was unjust and unreasonable, he approached the Alberta Union of Provincial Employees for assistance in a grievance process. Even though this bit of nastiness happened a few months before his long-planned retirement, his thoughts were with younger, less-experienced colleagues, a long way from retirement, with family, mortgages and long careers in front of them. It is of no small consequence if the pattern of bullying and intimidation persists, affecting resource professionals and their ability to manage natural resources in the public interest.

His persistence paid off and he was able to retire with a departmental acknowledgement of wrongdoing. Although there was never a formal apology, one never expects that from a bully. The acknowledgement of an inappropriate disciplinary action was a significant vindication of his stance, albeit at great personal cost. What John achieved with his stubborn adherence to principles is to have set the precedent that his remaining colleagues can stand behind.

## FIRE!!

The aphorism "Fire is a good servant, but a poor master" has multiple interpretations. The one clearest to me happened in the smoke of an escaped fire at a lake in the west country of Alberta. Now, fire in natural landscapes like forests is part of a normal ecological process, a way to renovate the forest, to reset the biological clock. My role in this fire might not have been considered part of "normal" processes. Everyone has the opportunity to light a fire, but once the spark has ignited, things can go dreadfully amiss.

My career aspiration was to become a biologist. I had landed a summer position with the Alberta Fish and Wildlife Division, working for Mel Kraft, in the old Red Deer Region. I couldn't get enough of it and volunteered one weekend to check on the status of the trout in Gap Lake, southwest of Nordegg. Golden trout, originally from the Sierra Nevada mountains of California, had been stocked in Gap Lake, following successful introductions in the Castle watershed. There had been concerns of winterkill. I was excited to have this task, and perhaps catch a golden trout.

In the days before off-highway vehicles were endemic and had taken over the forest reserves, this was a walk-in enterprise. I invited a friend to join me on an overnight backpack trip, coupled with some fishing. Although the distance into the lake was relatively short, it did entail hugging the east side of the valley, avoiding most wet meadows and muskegs.

I didn't think the hike too onerous, but Tom was of a different opinion. I thought he would have relished the walk.

I assumed that, as a hockey goalie, he would have been in shape. I was to learn that playing goalie was a mostly sedentary athletic pursuit, followed by beer. Tom was somewhat short and squat – deadfall that I walked over, he struggled with. We arrived at the lake – me exhilarated, him exhausted.

Gap Lake lies in a narrow, forested valley. Its origins may have been a rockslide across the valley, coupled with a beaver dam on a small stream that flows north to the North Saskatchewan River. At the north end of the lake was a grassy opening, beneath towering pines, a perfect camping spot. We heaved off our heavy packs, Tom collapsed, and I reconnoitred the site.

An old campfire ring was surrounded by knee-high grass. No one had camped there for several seasons and the old grass was thick and dry. I immediately recognized a hazard. We were going to cook over an open fire, so eliminating the risk of a wildfire, by burning a ring of dry grass to create a fire guard, seemed reasonable. The operative word was "reasonable." Maybe not prudent, as circumstances evolved.

I lit a match – there wasn't a puff of wind. Not even a gentle breeze to blow out the flame. I touched the match to the grass, and it ignited immediately, indicating how dry the thatch was.

Now, before God and three other responsible witnesses, I can say that from the time I lit that match and touched it to the grass, to full ignition, a stiff breeze intervened. That grass wanted, yearned, to burn and the flames took off, faster than I could imagine, propelled by a wind, suddenly from nowhere.

I want to make it clear I am not and have never been a pyromaniac (although my wife swears my eyes glaze over when I'm cutting firewood). As a kid I was repeatedly warned about playing with matches. My mother cautioned me that if a fire (of my origin) ever burned down the barn, that would be the end of the farm. We would be forced to live in a cardboard box and lick discarded gum wrappers for nourishment. She may not have said it in just that way, but the meaning was clear.

As a result, my forays into our woodlot to practise my wood-craft involved the cautious building of small fires to brew a billy can of tea. Not once did a fire ever escape the circle, and all were dead out and cold before I left the scene.

My fire prescription was exceeded in seconds. I grabbed my jacket and started to swat at the flames. Tom quickly revived and joined me. The grass fire thwarted our efforts and grew exponentially. Fire, if you view it dispassionately and from afar, is vibrantly alive. It eats fuel, excretes the waste as ash and breathes air just we do, sucking in oxygen and spewing out carbon dioxide. Fire grows, and as it spreads, it creates new fires that spread out and make new fires of their own.

The fire spread and ignited one of the lodgepole pines. A 12-metre pine exploded like a Roman candle in front of us. A blast of heat repelled us. Tom, ever the rational observer and master of understatement, commented, "I think this is beyond our control." At least he didn't make light of the situation by saying it was too bad we didn't have marshmallows – this was an amazing fire. I wouldn't have seen the humour in that!

Smoke billowed up, like thick cumulous clouds, obscuring the sky and enveloping us. This was not the mildly irritating smoke of a smouldering campfire. A dense pall of a viscous, hot and malevolent atmosphere surrounded us. A placid, sylvan lake scene was transformed in minutes into Dante's Inferno.

Not recognizing, perhaps in our dismay, that where there's fire, there's visible smoke, we decided we'd best alert the fire tower on Ram Mountain that our fire was out of control. This was in the golden era before cellphones, satellite phones or portable radios. So we began to run back to the truck, parked on the Meadows Road, to drive up and report the fire to the lookout stationed at Ram Mountain. I thought Tom would have a coronary on the jog out to the road, but he hung in with me, albeit with some difficulty. With a ragged breath he expressed his opinion that it was unlikely he would be joining me on other outings.

By the time we got to the tower, on a rough trail somewhat unsuitable for our two-wheel-drive vehicle, the lookout had already seen the smoke, identified the probable location and called in the cavalry. Ours was a completely redundant trip as Gap Lake lies immediately below Ram Mountain lookout. Often in the heat of the moment one fails to piece together the patently obvious.

We retraced our steps, ran back into Gap Lake, to find a minimum-security convict crew supervised by one forest ranger had beaten us to the punch. Tom again collapsed in the ashes of what would have been our camp. With introductions barely out of the way, we were nearly bombarded with a load of chemical fire retardant delivered by airplane. The red dust of the control agent sifted over the assembled group, colouring us all with the same hue, including the scorched and blackened meadow.

By this time it was evening, and with humidity levels rising, temperatures cooling and the wind dropping off to nearly calm, the ranger observed the fire was going nowhere. He decided that if the now smouldering fire was put out completely this would ruin an opportunity for a camp-out and overtime. We hunkered down for the night. *Hunker* is another operative word, one failing to fully describe our situation. The fire had burned not only away from the lake, pushed by the wind, but also back to the lake, where we had left our backpacks. Both were immolated, sleeping bags included.

As we shivered through the night, ironically without benefit of a warming fire, Tom reaffirmed his conviction that fighting a forest fire, jogs through the forest and slowly freezing to death were not on his radar when he agreed to join me. Although we remained lifelong friends until his passing a few years ago, we never rekindled such an adventure.

In the aftermath of this I thought my career was over, before it really began. My supervisor, Mel, brushed the incident aside, even though I'm sure there was pressure from the Forest Service to do otherwise. I know there were lots of snide comments about the "fisheries fire." These went up in smoke, literally, after a minimum-security crew, working under the supervision of the Forest Service, had a fire escape from brush piles being burned on Mount Baldy, across the river from Gap Lake. This blew into a large-scale wildfire that eclipsed my minor event. I did suffer the nickname "Torch" for a while.

Within a few years the Wildlife Branch initiated a controlled burn on the flanks of Ram Mountain to renovate mountain sheep range, turning forest back into grassland. This included the patch of burnt forest that ran up the mountain from Gap Lake. Wildlife staff remember the Forest Service equivocating over whether or not to light the fire. Conditions for controlled burns are rarely ever completely "right" for an over-cautious group with history of fighting fires, not lighting them. Over the radio was heard the suggestion the fire boss didn't have the "balls" to light the fire. He bristled and said, "I'll show you" and the smoke spiralled up over the making of new sheep range.

I was back at Gap Lake a few winters later to work on a habitat improvement project. The lake had winterkilled (the reason for my initial trip) and was likely to do so again, unless the water was deeper. A low-head dam would increase the lake level, but the surrounding perimeter of trees had to be removed, including the blackened pine skeletons resulting from my fire. All evidence was cut, piled and burned, albeit with an extreme hazard reduction of thick snow covering. No fire escaped.

I realized, in the context of both habitat improvement projects that benefited from my burn, that you can peak too early in your career, be too far ahead of the curve. There is a cost to innovation, even if it is a happy accident.

I think our past paranoia about fire and its control has exacerbated the situation we face today. Fire can be a tool, a good servant. Without its judicious use it can become the master, resulting in larger, more destructive conflagrations. But next time, someone else can light that match.

## BIOLOGISTS' ANGST

Two biologists from a consulting firm had asked to meet with me, as an oil company had hired them to discuss my concerns with a wellsite location on the headwaters of an Eastern Slopes trout stream. As I invited them into our boardroom, I noticed they were carrying a thin report. Some years previously I had done a comprehensive survey of the stream – physical habitat, aquatic invertebrates, water chemistry and trout population age and growth – and had used that information to register my concerns over the construction of a wellsite in the steep valley.

They began by asserting their results indicated there would be no concerns – no sediment, no disruption of stream flow, no leakage of drilling fluids, no change in trout habitat and no impacts on trout. To support this they handed me a thin report, a few pages at best, based on their assessment. I asked when they had done the work and how long it had taken. It had taken them an afternoon, on a short stretch of stream, to refute my findings and concerns. In response, I ripped the report in half and tossed it across the table!

This was not the first, nor would it be the last time in my career I observed (and experienced) the dilemma of biologists – the angst – that is part of the profession. The pro-development faction will hate you for rocking the boat and the environmental community will criticize you for not rocking it more. It is virtually impossible to find stable middle ground.

I recognize there may be a tendency for biologists to become cynical and pessimistic, with feelings of hopelessness, and finally giving up trying to make a difference. This comes with involvement with a score of bad land-use decisions, so much callous disregard for intact landscapes and wildlife and so many compromises that aren't really compromises but acquiescence to economic or political pressures. It is difficult, I know, to make yourself impervious to the losses, in situations where you are forced to surrender and then have to draft the terms of your surrender, in the form of hollow monitoring advice or empty mitigative solutions.

Going along to get along, drinking the purple Kool-Aid, and deceiving oneself that everything will work out (despite all evidence to the contrary) can be an outcome of the unrelenting pressures. The thing about going along to get along is, when you sup with the devil you need a very long spoon. At what point do you otherwise slide into the syndrome of "Well, it's going to happen anyway, so I might as well get on board?" The system, whether a government, corporate, academic or consulting one, produces an inexorable push in that direction, to become tied to the turning wheel.

One has to steel oneself, keeping ethics in the forefront, to tell truth to power (or a client), and suffer the possible repercussions. There are inevitable costs – a bureaucratic sense that you are not a "team player," difficult, uncompromising and certainly unsuited for advancement up the corporate food chain. It is an irony that many entities hire biologists, ostensibly to provide sound ecological advice, and then consistently ignore that advice and castigate the deliverer of the message.

In the development of survival skills some "street smarts" are in order. It's good to remind oneself that those who last and don't get fired have an opportunity to make real change, protect a little bit of Earth and its functions and creatures, and most importantly live to fight another day. But if you cross the line too often, subverting your ethics for a temporary strategic position, soon the line disappears.

To provide good advice, to maintain an ethical stance, requires the marshalling of evidence – the science. But in most circles and in many battles science isn't enough, especially when the debate is really over values.

This can be so in development projects focused on chancy economic return and high environmental costs. In these cases scientific evidence would expose the frailties in the project and, if the project is approved, increase the development and restoration price tag. It is here that pressure can be exerted to slant the evidence, come to a different conclusion, or use confirmation bias to select the references that support a particular outcome. When questioned in a survey, many Alberta biologists expressed that they had felt pressure to modify their results to meet with the wishes of a client, supervisor or senior bureaucrat.

In such cases the science comes under attack, as do the deliverers of it. Often, other practitioners of science will be employed to find the chinks in the armour of evidence, presenting their own, sometimes diametrically opposed interpretations and versions. Now this is fair, since science, everyone's, must stand up to review and scrutiny. This assumes that all regulatory hearings are fair, that decisions aren't already baked in, and the ultimate arbiters understand the science and aren't swayed with a disproportionate effort, funded by a well-heeled entity, creating a version of the interpretation that favours a proponent.

It might seem odd that often the interpretation of the data in the hands of biologists hired by a proponent is more positive about the development, less concerned about the impacts and leans more towards a reliance on mitigation or restoration. Are these biologists being enablers for their clients, or honest interpreters of the data?

This is where a more collegial system, rather than an adversarial one, would produce better decisions. What often needs review (and should be) is the professional code of conduct on the part of the collectors, interpreters and disseminators of biological evidence.

I worry that young biologists will take their obedient place in various bureaucracies and look to become successful cogs in the wheel – by letting the wheel spin them around as it wants without them taking a look at what they're doing. I hope that young (and not so young) biologists do not become passive acceptors of the official doctrine that economic development should not be questioned, examined and sometimes rejected. For, as Shirley Chisholm, an American politician, observed, "When morality comes up against profit, it is seldom that profit loses."

Ours is a world of economic giants and ethical infants. Aldo Leopold, the dean of ecological thinking, reflected on this with, "Ethical behaviour is doing the right thing when no one else is watching – even when doing the wrong thing is legal." In protecting the world for today and tomorrow, that is the choice for all biologists. I hope the two biologists, staring at their report torn in two, understood the message I had provided.

## A FROZEN HELL
### Descent into the Sheep River Canyon

The Lethe is the river of forgetfulness that runs through the Greek hell of Hades. In contrast, I can never forget the Sheep River, especially the descent into the frozen hell of its canyon in the spring of 1973.

When I returned from university in late April, Mel Kraft, the regional fisheries biologist, told me we were going down to the Sheep River to help Gerry Thompson. Gerry was working on his master's, investigating the biology and ecology of mountain whitefish. He had tagged fish and wanted to know if they were overwintering in the upper Sheep River. Mel said we would only be gone for a day as Gerry had assured him it was an easy one-day float, from Gorge Creek to Sandy McNabb campground, less than 20 kilometres. What Mel had neglected to ask was when Gerry had floated the canyon for that "easy one-day float."

We loaded up a 13-foot Boston Whaler boat, a generator, the electrofishing apparatus and other paraphernalia and headed south. Not expecting to be gone more than a day, we had the clothes on our backs and a lunch (as it turned out, not a big enough one).

Downstream of Gibraltar Mountain the Sheep River starts to incise, forming a steep-sided canyon often over a hundred metres deep that persists until just upstream of Turner Valley. As it carves its way downward, there are places where the backbone of the mountains will not break. The river has patience on its side, sandpapering and polishing the bedrock. Resistance is futile but the bedrock budges minimally, over the kind of time we cannot fathom.

Entering the dark canyon, only dimly lit by the spring sun, seemed like a trip into the bowels of the Earth, highlighted by the frozen springs and seeps on the canyon walls. The river level was low; no spring melt had started. It looked like an easy float, for a day of fisheries exploration.

Then we came to our first ice bridge. Earlier, higher flows had frozen, creating bridges of ice across the channel. We were to encounter many of these, often a metre thick and suspended above the water one to three metres. Suddenly the trip took on an aspect of polar exploration, if not something akin to the

Franklin expedition. The electrofishing equipment, with a generator and other gear, was floated in a fibreglass boat – the combination weighed close to a ton. Unloading equipment, then heaving a heavy boat onto the ice and back down, over and over, consumed much of the day and much energy.

The routine was to get the boat as close to the edge of the ice as we could, then pass the pieces of equipment to someone on the ice bridge. Then two people would lift the bow high enough for the other two on the ice to grab it. With luck, then two of us would push from the stern as the others would tug at the bow and it would slide on top of the ice.

Except, sometimes the ice bridge was across a pool, too deep to wade. We would float to the edge and clamber up the sheer face, with others pushing to give momentum to get someone on top. Sometimes it worked. When it didn't, someone would have to shimmy across the rock face trying to find toeholds with our inadequate mountaineering chest waders.

The person on top would secure the boat with a rope and then the arduous process of transferring equipment would begin. With all the gear up top, then everyone else would follow. Grabbing the rope, we would all pull, with all our might, to slowly slide the boat up too. The bow would often stick, so one of us would have to push the bow out while the rest of us pulled. There were many times we would have had to abandon the boat were it not for Mel's brute strength.

The footing was incredibility treacherous. Compared to modern waders, especially those with carbide studs that grip slippery rock, the waders of the day were rubber-soled with minimal traction. Trying to stay upright on a piece of stream-polished rock or on rounded boulders, while attempting to catch a fish with a dip net, was like dancing on greased cannonballs. You might get a pirouette or two in before heading for an impromptu bath. We would stop, empty our waders of water just a notch or two above being solid, wring out our socks, and continue the march. Bruises added up and our feet took the brunt of collisions with rocks and boulders through the thin material of the waders.

The process of lift, drag, splash down and continue went on until nearly dusk, when Gerry finally indicated we were a long way from the exit point. At this point he also confessed he had floated the section in the summer!

This required a retreat, leaving the gear behind – it was in no danger of being stolen. Climbing the canyon walls in near darkness, clad in chest waders, was an experience not to be recommended. Some of the seeps had frozen and parts of the canyon walls were ice covered. Ken Crutchfield was working in the area, and when Mel and I arrived at his trailer door, wet, tired and very, very hungry, he fed us a gargantuan dinner, plied us with rum (for medicinal purposes) and tucked us into bed.

In morning light the canyon did not look quite as daunting, until we started down. As it turned out, climbing up was a breeze compared to a barely controlled descent to the river.

The next day was more of the same, ice bridges one after another, being constantly wet, and morale had dropped to the mutiny level. By late afternoon even Gerry's usual optimistic nature had evaporated, and he signalled we needed to get out before the river claimed us, by dark. Not arguing and without bothering to electrofish anymore, we pushed onward.

Our retreat was a blur of more obstacles, now including bedrock chutes and small waterfalls. At one water-polished bedrock chute Gerry, guiding the boat through it, slipped. His feet went out from under him and as he went down his waders ballooned full with water, sucking him under the boat. I turned at an opportune moment and could only see his hand still clutching the grab rail on the stern.

By this time we were all exhausted, probably hypothermic, and Gerry's summer assistant, Paul, lay down on a gravel bar. "Just leave me here to die," he said, in a plaintive voice. We weren't sure whether or not to take him seriously. But he could die later, on his own time, because we needed all hands on deck.

As it turned out we floated the last piece in the dark, another experience not to be recommended. If a nighttime float had a virtue it was you didn't need to fret about the upcoming obstacles because you couldn't see (or feel) them until the last moment.

The mountain whitefish? We caught a handful (11), dispelling the theory the canyon was their overwintering lair. We tried to rationalize that the absence of whitefish was still important biological data. Tough field days were traded for scraps of invaluable knowledge about creatures that don't give up their secrets easily.

Still in our wet clothes, Mel and I loaded up and headed back to Red Deer. We stopped in Calgary for a steak dinner, completely blowing our meal per diem. One steak didn't seem like enough. We arrived back home about 2 a.m., in an era where no one paid attention to overtime hours.

Some time later I was reading Gerry's master's thesis and I noticed in the acknowledgements he had thanked Mel and his "electrofishing crew." For all that effort I never got name recognition! Gerry did apologize for that oversight.

The descent into the Sheep River canyon became my litmus test. No matter how difficult a task was – as cold, wet, miserable, scared and uncomfortable as I could be – none of those incidents were ever as bad as the Sheep River trip. As the axiom goes, what doesn't kill you makes you stronger.

## HARD WORDS FOR TROUBLED TIMES

Things that matter do not come easily, seamlessly or without effort and persistence. It is such with protecting the environment. It takes a great deal of courage to say "no" to the prevailing fashions and fascinations with our economically driven age, or the presuppositions that this is the way it should and has to be.

As E.F. Schumacher, author of *Small Is Beautiful*, observed, "Call a thing immoral or ugly, soul-destroying or a degradation to man, a peril to the peace of the world or to the well-being of future generations: as long as you have not shown it to be 'uneconomic' you have not really questioned its right to exist, grow, and prosper."

The requisite strength to speak out and up is derived from deep convictions. A society driven by greed loses the ability to see things in context and is incapable of discerning the unfortunate outcomes of precipitous actions. Herman Daly, an economist with a soul, says, "The current national accounting system [GDP] treats the earth as a business in liquidation."

In Alberta we've liquidated most of the native grasslands, with a rich diversity of plants and animals, transforming them into monocultures of barley and canola. Southern Alberta's rivers are running dry with the demands of irrigation agriculture.

A frantic rush to deplete petroleum resources leaves an indelible mark on the landscape and contributes to our climate change woes. Our forests have been "scientifically" manipulated to form crops, ignoring watershed values, fish and wildlife habitats and recreational havens. If that isn't enough, despite a world turning its back on coal, there seems to be a coal-rush for metallurgical coal resources in the Eastern Slopes. This has the potential to poison the water and the air, eliminate native trout populations and turn off a magnet for tourism and recreation.

We need to ask some impertinent questions about these economic schemes and dreams. Who benefits? Who pays? What is the time frame? Where are the supporting data? How objective are the impact assessments? What are the consequences? What are the alternatives? And the most telling question – just because we can do something, should we? The compass of compassion asks not how much we can grab, but how much we should leave.

A major criticism of those who question these economic dreams is that they ask nagging questions focusing on the ecological costs and consequences of an economic activity. Conversely, the propensity of politicians, corporations and promoters is to extol and overinflate the benefits, often with questionable math projections and dismiss, out of hand, any environmental issues. There is a tendency to glibly assert that any environmental issues can be easily and cheaply mitigated, most often without supporting evidence.

Ironically, now banks, investors and insurance companies are asking the same nagging questions, because of better understanding of uncertainty, risk, dubious benefits and mounting environmental costs/liabilities from unsustainable and poorly scoped ventures.

Wendell Berry's conclusion and guidance is, "We have lived our lives by the assumption that what was good for us would be good for the world. We have been wrong. We must change our lives so that it will be possible to live by the contrary assumption, that what is good for the world will be good for us. And that requires that we make the effort to know the world and learn what is good for it."

Concerned citizens should reject the assumption that it is easier to dream than to unseat a culture drunk on plenty, impatient with restrictions and determined to wring more from the landscape than can be done sustainably. When governments, corporations and individuals act selfishly, rapaciously and impetuously, all of us should feel obligated to speak out.

The imposed dichotomy between the economy and the environment needs desperately to be exposed. Economic arguments must be made that are robust enough to survive when pinned up against the tree of ecology. This is the straw man of empirical analysis – posit the proposal, and then let it respond to the withering blasts of reality. This is how science proceeds. So too do wise societies and civilizations.

The carefree good times are gone – we've exhausted the possibilities that gave us the good times and they won't return. That is the situation everywhere. There are no new frontiers left to exploit (other than the questionable madness of space exploration) to buy us more time (or more stuff).

It's best to consider what we have left, marshal those opportunities and steward them more carefully, with a longer-term vision. We could still be considered lucky by others in the world not so fortunate. We can be smart and live reasonably well for the foreseeable future, or continue to be profligately wasteful and stupid, cratering over the short term.

*Illustration by Liz Saunders*

# 8
# Meditations

*The world is so constructed that if you wish to enjoy its pleasures, you must also endure its pain. Whether you like it or not, you cannot have one without the other.*

—Brahmanandam

## THINKING LIKE A LEOPOLD

To say Aldo Leopold was the dean of ecologists, the father of wildlife management and the torchbearer for wilderness might seem presumptuous, but he was all that, and more.

I never had the opportunity to meet Aldo Leopold. He died, too early, two years before I was born. I didn't encounter him until about 1968 when I picked up a slim volume of *A Sand County Almanac* in a university library. That tiny paperback still sits in my bookshelf. I hope the statute of limitations has run out on my failure to return it. In my defence, I have read, reviewed and referred to it more than any other book I've owned. It allowed me to get to know and appreciate the philosophy and wisdom of Aldo Leopold.

His ability to draw lessons from circumstances and experiences, to admit having made mistakes and to convey messages on conservation in an easily accessible form is a strength found in all of his writings. And so, as many read the Bible, I read Aldo Leopold. I find truth, inspiration and timelessness in his words.

Another bit of understanding of his success at writing so clearly on conservation came to me on the visit to the "shack," the Leopold family refuge in one of the "sand" counties of Wisconsin. The shack was an old chicken coop converted into a cabin on worn-out, orphaned land adjacent to the Wisconsin River.

I visited the shack on April 1. As Mark Twain recounted, "This is the day upon which we are reminded of what we are on the other three hundred and sixty-four." I didn't feel foolish but rather felt I was on my way to a shrine, as important to me as Mecca is to Muslims and the Vatican is to Catholics.

From the original 80 acres the tract has grown to over 200 acres, administered by the Sand County Foundation. There was no sign, no memorial and no one else at the laneway off Rustic Road 49, but I saw the shape of a building beneath the forest canopy at the end of the narrow trail. Snow fell, big flakes at first, then turning to pellets that ricocheted off the dry oak leaves.

The shack sits on the edge of an open field of restored native grass, beneath a canopy of large pines. It is unassuming, even undistinguished, with weathered boards, just a slight step above its beginnings as a chicken coop. Amenities are non-existent, and it is like stepping back in time to a rudimentary homestead of the early part of the 20th century. Logs, planks and simple benches are arrayed around the yard – just the venue for camp-fire discussions on conservation issues, I think.

Faint goose music echoed, amid the traffic noise from nearby Interstate 90. Fox sparrows and juncos scratched in the openings and, when alarmed, flew into the thick tangles of underbrush and vines. Snow started to accumulate and I left, reluctantly. I was surprised to see that two hours had gone by while I absorbed and meditated. I didn't feel the time slipping by.

No, Aldo Leopold did not speak to me. But the spirit of the place did. At the shack I sensed awareness that science and conservation are nourished by a personal contact with the soil, the landscape and wild creatures. From this humble place worn out by greed and neglect, Leopold, a patient observer, discerned cycles, patterns, associations, linkages, connections and truths. The place remains part laboratory, part classroom, surely a memorial and still a landscape in transition from the bootlegger who exploited the land and trees and then dumped it back on the county, taxes unpaid, before Leopold's family purchased it in the early 1930s.

I have the Sierra Club reprint of Leopold's classic, initially published in 1949 ($0.95). "Classic" is the appropriate term, since *A Sand County Almanac* is a work that never loses its influence or relevance. It has been read, then reread, and the messages flowed from it as I gained an appreciation of the import of the words, stories, layers, metaphors and teachings. The book is now well-thumbed, dog-eared and taped together, with passages on virtually every page underlined and highlighted. It's full of marginal notes, many from other Leopold sources. And I still find new treasures, new explanations hidden in the passages every time I turn the pages. Leopold's words sparked early inspiration and over time enriched it with subtle wisdom.

Leopold's body of work in *A Sand County Almanac* has been described as an amalgam of ethics, esthetics and ecology – alliterative and unifying. As a biologist, early ecologist, teacher, philosopher and writer, he drew on his keen observations of landscapes, wildlife and people to address the issues he saw confronting and confounding conservation. I am in awe of his writing style, the clarity, brevity and simple elegance of expression. What is equally evident, and profound, is that his observations, conclusions and wisdom are as relevant today as they surely were decades ago when he put his pen to paper.

It's hard not to be moved by his convention of conveying truths through stories. Stories still have a power to communicate, even to unreceptive minds in today's fractured social-media world. His stories are circular, and work on many levels and senses. They engage to find common ground, and despite our electronic and digital worlds we have not yet lost the genetic hard-wiring to listen to stories. Nor should we, I think. The universe is made of stories, not atoms, said someone wise. History might record, and I believe Leopold thought, that monumental changes are only possible when the stories people tell each other about the world generate a critical mass of awareness. With awareness comes understanding, and once you know, there is an obligation to act.

Leopold's writings are my philosophical touchstone, a place to reaffirm my position and obligations. His words are also a constant reminder that he took risks, based on carefully thought-through principles. When he was wrong he said so, and used the example to indicate we should never hew to orthodoxy in our thinking. The maintenance of our world, the natural one that supports the economic and social interests of the human-contrived one, requires the courage to speak up.

We could stand the advice and perspectives from more Aldo Leopolds, especially over billionaire robber barons, ecologically illiterate politicians and an economic system predicated on constant growth over sustainability.

Leopold has helped and continues to help me in moments of uncertainty, in episodes of controversy and in margins of isolation to persist. I believe, as I think he did, that skilled advocacy in the public arena, aided by information from specialists, will advance progress towards a world Leopold envisioned – one where we realize we are part of the land and have obligations to that which supports us.

With my writing I pay homage to the memory of Aldo Leopold. It is a far better thing, however, for us in our lives to pay homage to him in the most effective way – by ensuring that our landscapes, water and wildlife are shaped by his ideals.

## AT FIRST LIGHT

No photograph could have captured it, although in the memory the nuances of light, dark, shadow, texture and colour remain. A painter might have done a tolerable job. That assumes the palate was expressive enough to include the cerebral sense of warmth with sunrise, coupled with the visceral, bone-chilling cold of an air temperature well below freezing. It would have been a curious juxtaposition if the oils had remained viscous or the watercolours unfrozen.

A video could have done some justice to the creeping potential of dawn and the explosion of light as the sun crested the ridge to the east. It might have encapsulated a segment, a vignette of motion and the sense of time. That is, if the hands would have been steady enough, or the fingers sufficiently thawed and flexible to focus the camera. A big if, I think.

A photographic image, even a painting, can recall, like an imperfect sketch, what one saw. This gives rise to memory and a spark to our brain's hard drive to resurrect all the senses of the scene. We then try to recreate not just what was seen, but the richer, multi-dimensional tapestry of what we felt and experienced.

It's best to be aware of our limitations with words and pictures. Despite our skills and the artifacts of our art, we cannot hope to match, to recreate, the throb of life, the panorama that unfolds before us and the intangible, uncapturable qualities of the phases, faces and moods of the landscape.

I took no pictures, nor did I sketch the scene that cold, clear fall day at dawn. Sometimes it is a distraction to attempt to record a scene instead of just watching and participating in it. Not only do we lack the technology to capture the essence of a scene, but we also can't often define or divine the meaning. There it is, and it is beautiful. That's enough. Better perhaps to be part of it all than to parse it into bits for analysis.

Only in memory are found all the indelible features, images and senses of that morning. In the senescence of autumn, the grass held variegated shades, from gold through tan to brown.

Each blade of grass was rimmed with frost – thick hoarfrost layered to provide individual definition. Each frost crystal was an individual prism funnelling, focusing and refracting light. Rays of sunlight bent and split into a kaleidoscope of colour with the jewelling of each frost particle as the sun washed over the field of grass. No wind betrayed this decoration.

No human ingenuity could have eclipsed this scene or even matched or paralleled it. This was real special effects, organic and natural. It's a time when you catch yourself forgetting to breathe. Scenes like this quicken the heart, like glimpsing the face of a lovely woman in a crowd. The encounter occurs in seconds, maybe less, but the heart is filled with wonder, delight and joy.

There are those rare moments of such sublime delight you want them to endure, but they don't, and that may be their virtue. For if they lasted too long the risk increases that they would become common, mundane and not powerful enough to provoke a memory. A snapshot is what we get – and if we are receptive and watchful that is reward enough.

On the eastern horizon clouds had lifted slightly, providing a window through which sunlight poured, bathing the scene. Light at dawn and dusk has a special quality – warmer, diffuse, oblique and expressive. Maybe it's related to the anticipation of a day after a period of darkness, or a day ending, soon to be plunged into gloom again, that gives this brief period an intrinsic but hard-to-describe feeling. Ephemeral and fleeting, perhaps, but tangible to the eye.

Four white-tailed does emerge or, it seems to the senses, materialize, apparate from out of a patch of aspen. Their backs are blanketed in frost, reminding me of the comfort of earlier wood heat and a down sleeping bag. As they cautiously advance, their legs scatter jewels of ice, and the sunlight bounces off puffs of frost dust. Deer eyes are brown, liquid, and have the catch light of the recently risen sun reflected. Brown on white is the palate. The image is reminiscent of a ship on a winter north Atlantic run – ice encrusted on top, rusty brown beneath and white waves below the Plimsoll line.

All creation, embodied at that moment in those four deer. They could be an apt metaphor for the true grandeur of life, especially on such a morning. For it is on occasions such as this that there is a palpable sense of being part of it all, and because of the connection, responsible.

They come closer, unsuspecting but alert. Evolution with predators gives them a constant aura of vigilance. Be still, I think, and ignore your toes that scream to move and allow some hot blood to circulate to them. Consciousness seeps into my mind at about the same rate of blood flow to my toes. It is about the wonder, promise and reward of being present at first light.

## CORNERS AND FENCEROWS

Weathered, split cedar posts in a fence corner of introduced brome grass, all dating from our homestead history. Rusted, busted, obsolete and abandoned farm equipment piled into the corner, out of the way of the cultivated field. The fence corner and its accumulation of agricultural flotsam and jet-sam is the only uncultivated space in a seeming eternity of canola stubble.

Yet, on the edge are the dusting depressions and droppings from birds, sharp-tailed grouse maybe. More likely the spoor of pheasants, another non-native added to the mix. It is in these edges, abandoned corners, weedy fencerows and ground too rocky to cultivate where one pursues game birds, trying to shut out the overwhelming picture of a landscape transformed in a little over a century to a manipulated human canvas.

The dog doesn't care – his world is one of scent, and the wisps of wind tell him these islands hold birds. He would argue sight isn't the best faculty to have when one walks these field edges.

Rusted barbed wire drapes loosely from one cedar post to another. At the rate of metal deterioration, the cedar will out-live the wire stapled loosely to each post. In this dry climate of southern Alberta maybe the posts will survive us. They certain-ly have outlived those who planted them in this hard ground almost a century ago.

In the season of autumn, the palate is monochromatic – tans and browns. As the dog moves through the cover, he trig-gers an explosion of colour, of reds, black, gold and white, with purplish and green iridescence. A pheasant, a rooster, flushes from beneath his inquiring nose. The colour combination is the antithesis of that of the cover he hides in, yet he has been completely concealed from my view. Only the dog knew he was there and prodded him into a vivid kaleidoscope of bril-liant flight.

The pheasant disappears, immune from my shotgun blast. The dog looks on, somewhat disapprovingly, and continues down the fencerow. But he is not one for recriminations and lectures. When you live in the moment, as a dog does, you dwell on what's in front of you, not what has passed into history.

Maybe this bit of dog philosophy would help us all, especially those who mourn for landscapes lost, irrevocably damaged, bereft of any wild aspect or the indicators of wildness, like wild-life. A dog might counsel us to move on. There's birds ahead; let's anticipate the next fence corner.

It's time, a dog might reflect, to nourish the soul and ignore, at least for the moment, the scars, blemishes and warts of our overzealous economic endeavours. Not a long-term strategy, but good enough for a walk along a fencerow, between the corners. Time enough to leave the dream of a more intact, connected and diverse landscape filled with birds to another moment.

## EATING TOMORROW

It was a sight to behold, and one greater to comprehend the eating of, that chocolate cream pie. We had whipped it together from graham cracker crumbs and chocolate pudding, shaken and then chilled in a snowbank on a backpacking trip.

The anticipation of eating it brought me back to the level of a child, thinking only of immediate gratification. My two companions showed considerably more restraint, electing to divide each of their respective thirds in half, to have a piece at breakfast the next morning. I ate my third immediately. The saved piece of pie was enclosed in a rock cairn to protect it from marauders. I was teased unmercifully about how good the remainder would taste in the morning, had I saved some of my pie.

The early glow of morning light revealed the cairn had been transformed into a scatter of rocks. No pie remains were left and the aluminum pie plate retained gouges on its surface. A mule deer doe was beating a hasty retreat from the scene, saving me from instant suspicion.

But a closer inspection of the scene, with all the intensity of a Crime Scene Investigation unit, showed a porcupine was the culprit. Somewhere in the headwaters of the Castle River there may well be a line of porcupines still hard-wired to remember a meal of non-wood, chocolate ambrosia tinged with a slight metallic aftertaste.

It was my turn to laugh, since I had lost nothing in this porcupine-perpetrated crime. The moral of the story, I pontificated, was that "gluttony is its own reward." Saving a piece of the pie was foolish, because how could we predict the events of the future, and indeed the tragic loss of the saved pie? Eating it all now was the smart thing to do.

It was only later, upon reflection, that I realized how much the incident revealed of human nature. In our province and country – indeed, on our continent if not worldwide – there is a similar orthodoxy, verging on a religion, that governs economic development. Its mantra goes something like "we can do everything, everywhere, anytime, all the time, at the same time, on the same place." It is a mantra that aptly describes ongoing trends in resource-rich provinces and states, including our own, where our drive for growth far exceeds our willingness to protect species at risk.

Aren't we remarkable? We make the common rare; the rare endangered; and the endangered are – lost. It would be more remarkable, maybe in the category of miraculous, to reverse that process.

On and on it goes, despite the persistent signs of stress, of landscapes unravelling and of species driven to the category of "imperilled," or worse, "gone." If the public's overarching goal is to keep the engines of industry revved up and redlined on growing economic activity, then we are condemned to living in a fool's paradise. That would be a place where we continue to tinker, fiddle, adjust, redial, patch over, prevaricate, deny and generally ignore the signs until it's too late.

It is frustrating to sit on species recovery teams and note the intransigence, even belligerence, of industry and the timidity of government over protection and restoration of species at risk and their critical habitats. Equally unsettling, there appears to be little energy and few resources left to keep other species, like pronghorn antelope as an example, from joining the list of the damned. We need the equivalent of a Schindler's list for critters that may be on the brink of a downward spiral, and an accompanying hero to rescue them.

Our Alberta canaries are caribou, grizzlies, sage-grouse, cutthroat trout and the numerous, non-charismatic, micro fauna and flora on the growing list of species at risk. We think, when one of those canaries dies, we can simply buy another. We don't grasp, metaphorically, what the canary represents. It is an opportunity to use a sensitive or indicator species as a distant early warning system to alert us, to signal problems we, as humans, will eventually encounter. If the canary, metaphorical or otherwise, dies, it's too late. We've missed, ignored or over-ridden the signal at that point.

The problem is, many of us aren't clear on where you go to buy more actual Alberta canaries like caribou, grizzlies, sage-grouse, cutthroat trout and the numerous, non-charismatic, micro fauna and flora on the growing list of species at risk. There's no address on Google Maps for the endangered species store, and even if there were such a mythical place, I'll bet they don't take credit cards. At least, I'll bet, they won't take a credit card from the province of Alberta because our account is already overdrawn at the biodiversity bank.

Once they're gone, it's too late to dial back, ease the throttle of progress back a hair from redline, point fingers or wring our collective hands and promise it will never happen again. As Aldo Leopold correctly observed, "A little repentance just before a species goes over the brink is enough to make us feel virtuous. When the species is gone, we have a good cry and repeat the performance."

So why, one might ask, is the performance repeated? Species missing in action is a consequence of our turning their essential habitats into battle zones of industrial, agricultural or residential activity. At a frantic pace of development, both spatially and temporally, many native species lose out in the race. It isn't a race they have run before. It isn't a race they *can* run. The focus on purely economic outputs divides and transforms habitats into smaller and smaller units, fragmenting them, severing connections, reducing quality until those habitats no longer meet the needs of native plants, animals and fish.

Economists use a term "discounting the future" to describe the phenomenon where rewards in the present, the now, are valued more highly than rewards in the distant future. I suppose that as individuals and as society we find it difficult to delay gratification. We think it imperative to clutch and grab as much as we can now.

To eat the chocolate cream pie now is better than the prospect of having a piece in the future, or so goes the thought process. That process continues, to the point where a barrel of oil, a bushel of canola or a truckload of dimensional lumber provides more security now than the future prospect of these commodities plus fresh, abundant water supplies, healthy landscapes, the full expression of biodiversity and the delivery of ecosystem services.

Wade Davis, an Explorer-in-Residence of the National Geographic Society from 2000 to 2013, points out, "The cost of destroying a natural asset or its inherent worth if left intact has no metric in the economic calculations that support the industrialization of the wild. As long as there is the promise of revenue flows and employment, it merely requires permission to proceed. We take this as a given for it is the foundation of our system, the way commerce extracts value and profit in a resource-driven economy."

The cost of exercising all our options now is lost or missed opportunities and options for the future. Many natural assets can slip through the cracks because of a failure to value them appropriately. We "eat our future," as Australian biologist Tim Flannery observes. What develops is a syndrome of fire sale clearances on certain resources, at a reduced value, with little insight into how use could be sustainable with the maintenance of other resource values. In the race to grab it all now there are losers. The discount produces a dichotomy between those whose goal is short-term reward and those with a longer view and concern about future conditions. It is also a mockery of our rhetoric about conservation and stewardship.

Now I regret the gluttony of eating all of my pie at once, without a thought for tomorrow!

## PUTTING A LANDSCAPE TO "WORK"

Listening to some planners, loggers, corporate executives and bureaucrats, you would think landscapes are "lazy" if they are not "working," as in a "working landscape." Honestly, it paints a picture of a bunch of indolent landscapes lounging on a couch, remote control in hand, drinking beer and eating chips. They just lie there, capturing and storing water, transferring solar energy into plant growth, building soil, creating space and opportunity for biodiversity, and a bunch of other slothful activities.

Apparently, that's not enough. Landscapes have to "pay the rent," be contributing members of our society, meeting our varied economic, social, recreational and cultural wants. They have to make a living, hold down a job, as we can't have a bunch of ne'er-do-well landscapes dragging down the GDP. How would it look to the neighbours?

Working landscapes with logging, mining, agriculture, oil and gas, motorized recreation, random camping, fishing, hunting and hiking, with a healthy dollop of tourism development thrown in for good measure are, to some, ideal. That's a landscape that has pulled itself up by its own bootstraps, one to be admired, emulated, instead of those parks and protected areas thought of by some as wasted space.

The term is often code for "multiple use," itself a euphemism for "multiple abuse." These tend to be landscapes where we cram too much activity onto a finite land base by doing everything, everywhere, all the time, any time.

Maybe these should be called "indentured" landscapes – slaves to our wants and needs, heedless of the cost of overuse and indifferent to the inherent values. Our language, especially the choice of the word "working," may undercut our ability and will to manage and respect a landscape for the countless things it does for us, over and above our own selfish aspirations. Those are the things it does for us and society in its current lazy state.

Do we need to whip every landscape into increased economic productivity, at the expense of many ecosystem goods and services? When the whip marks are evident, like a loss of native vegetation, erosion and weeds, those are some signals that we have achieved a "working landscape."

More appropriately, others describe a working landscape in more meaningful terms. Working Landscapes, a not-for-profit organization in North Carolina, describes these as "places that work," economically, environmentally and socially. The setting is a productive landscape where farms, forests and small towns all contribute to a vibrant economy and community. Contextually, these landscapes are healthy in terms of environmental and human health. These are places where it is recognized that opportunity exists in natural, cultural and human assets – "an authentic landscape."

The antithesis is, as author and professor Peter Cannavò describes, places where "rampant development, unsustainable resource exploitation, and commodification ruin both natural and built landscapes, disconnecting us from our surroundings and threatening our fundamental sense of place."

In conservation a conflict has developed between development and preservation, often stated in terms of "parks vs. playgrounds," "economy vs. environment," and "people vs. protection." The conflict creates a "crisis of place," especially with islands of parks and protected areas that are isolated from each other.

"Place" is not an object, not a foundation of raw resources for solely economic endeavour, and for manipulation for primarily human wants and desires. It is the recognition of a coherent, enduring and valuable landscape in its own right, where development requires integration with preservation. It is not the piling on of more development and saying we will somehow mitigate our inability to set thresholds and limits.

Wendell Berry summarizes it this way: "Whereas the exploiter asks of a piece of land only how much and how quickly it can be made to produce, the nurturer asks a question that is much more complex and difficult: What is its carrying capacity?"

To achieve real working landscapes, we need to see them as places where we humans work as responsible members of a natural landscape, not as owners, extractors and short-term renters. Working landscapes should thrive under human influence where our needs are met (and moderated) in ways that maintain the landscape and landscape functions. "Mutual sustainability" should be the goal and test of a working landscape.

Not all landscapes are true working landscapes, and care needs to be taken to avoid the use of the term to subvert and diminish non-human values in favour of development. A thousand-acre canola field with no fencerows, no wetlands, no intact riparian areas, nor any vestige of natural vegetation is not a working landscape. Nor is an industrial complex, a mine site, an industrial logging clear-cut or urban sprawl. These are "worked on" and "worked over" landscapes, akin to being taken on by a prize fighter. While they provide economic and, to a lesser extent, social benefits, many if not most ecological values have been sacrificed.

Marjorie Kinnan Rawlings, Pulitzer Prize–winning American author, provided something to consider when she said: "It seems to me that the earth may be borrowed but not bought. It may be used, but not owned. It gives itself in response to love and tending, offers its seasonal flowering and fruiting. But we are tenants and not possessors, lovers and not masters."

In *A Sand County Almanac*, Aldo Leopold addressed the issue with this: "The land-relation is still strictly economic, entailing privileges but not obligations." In the Foreword of his book Leopold wrote: "We abuse land because we regard it as a commodity belonging to us. When we see land as a community to which we belong, we may begin to use it with love and respect."

The words of Leopold and Rawlings provide us with the best sense of what a working landscape is and how to measure whether we are tenants or masters of the landscape.

## IF THE HOUSE IS BURNING, SHOULD YOU YELL "FIRE!"?

My churchgoing friends point out that the Old Testament of the Bible is filled with fire, brimstone and liberal amounts of damnation. By contrast, the New Testament is kinder and gentler, with the option of redemption. It strikes me that this dichotomy is analogous to the divide between the strident voices of environmental apocalypse and those preaching that either there is no immediate problem or that salvation through technological alternatives and opportunities will keep us from cratering.

A colleague whose opinion I value provided some feedback on a piece detailing the dismal state of environmental affairs. He made the point that yelling "Fire!" without providing solutions just makes people tune out. Another, lecturing university students, noticed that a constant barrage of bad news on environmental issues caused many eyes in the class to glaze over.

So this raises the question: If something like the environment is burning, when is it okay to yell "Fire!"?

In "Wetlands," an essay in the appropriately titled book *Burning Questions*, Margaret Atwood points out that she is often accused of being harsh in speaking on environmental issues. She writes:

> So harsh, to wake sleepwalkers from their trance. Everyone would be rather told that things are fine, the world is safe, we're all nice people, and nothing is anyone's fault – after all, that we can keep on doing exactly what we like, without taking any thought or changing our so-called lifestyle in the least, and there will be no bad consequences...Trouble is, it's not true. So maybe it's time to be a little harsh. The situation we find ourselves in cannot be dealt with through anything less than plain speaking.

To those pinning their hopes on technology, on incremental behavioural shifts and on vague policy pronouncements with even vaguer timelines for implementation, I say I hope time is on our side. Many "solutions" are too small in scale, unproven, lack universal application, or are "greenwashing" to provide the illusion of success. Most experts agree we had a long time to prepare – and we didn't.

Unfortunately, without meaningful action, things may end up badly. W.C. Fields, the American comedian and acknowledged atheist, was found reading the Bible near his death. When asked of the apparent contradiction his reply was, "Looking for loopholes, looking for loopholes." No loopholes will substitute for a change in our habits.

Then there are those outright deniers of issues and the prevaricators, especially the industries that have given us irremediable pollutants, irrevocably damaged landscapes and watersheds and the global spectre of climate change. The petroleum industry has the dubious distinction of being at the head of the pack in regard to these issues. Many of their proposed solutions are about as useful as a glass hammer. One petroleum spokesman pointed out the specious logic that more development was necessary to provide resources to government to fund the restoration of the historic industry footprint.

I don't believe or accept that all of the problems we face, alone or in combination, are insoluble. But they will be unless we goad, encourage and motivate people into action. That won't necessarily happen with a soft soap approach. Why? Because we don't like, appreciate or embrace change willingly. And change is what is desperately needed.

There comes a time when it is necessary to scare the crap out of people, so they face the issues squarely and are unable to wriggle off the hook of responsibility and accountability. If a substance or an activity will surely kill you if you are unaware and take no precautions, it would seem logical to be straight up about the implications of ignoring the peril.

Mark Twain might have been thinking about this when he said, "A newspaper is not just for reporting the news, it's to get people mad enough to do something about it."

Sometimes it takes strong views to advance discussion, or even debate and challenge the comfortable thought that things will go on as they always have and change is unnecessary. Detractors of this use words like inflammatory, controversial, hyperbolic, provocative and apocalyptic to douse the fervour of those concerned with imminent environmental collapse.

Each of us has our own red line – that point at which the limits of patience and optimism have been breached and you can no longer convince yourself that everything will be fine, and things will get better if you just wait a little longer.

Then the only option is to yell "Fire!"

## AN ECOLOGIST'S PRAYER

As we stumble through today's world, between the immensities of life and the trivialities of living, help us recognize the gifts of this Earth. Help us create more understanding than anger, dispense more empathy than derision, and spread more hope than despair.

Never let us become so indifferent that we fail to see the wonder in a child's eyes of a bird in flight, or to listen to the wisdom of someone old recalling prior times. Never let us forget that our total effort is to help people see this place called Earth as home, steer them to recognize the limits of this place and to appreciate that each generation owes a debt to the next one. Never let us forget that together we can do these essential tasks.

The natural world holds much joy, satisfaction, rewards and learning. Knowing about, caring for and acting to protect, restore and manage the place that sustains us is a fundamental responsibility. We need to begin those conversations about breaking new ground and finding common ground for stewardship. Breaking bread together might be the finest way to have those conversations. When we are about to eat let us remember it is a gift and not forget to give thanks to a benevolent Earth for the meal.

## WHAT DO WILD PLACES MEAN?

It was a trail that defied gravity. As I slogged up it, one painful step after another, water leaked out of me at a rate faster than replacement. At a pass where the panorama spread out beneath my feet, all thoughts of fatigue disappeared. Drinking in the view, almost by osmosis, and leaning against a lichen-encrusted boulder was rejuvenating. It was also distracting, so much so that the storm caught us all unawares.

Some powerful entity dimmed the switch on daylight, and the dark clouds poured through the jagged spine of an arête like smoke boiling out of an industrial smokestack. Thunder punctuated the need to get off the high ground, and quickly. In rapid succession the wind whipped downslope, bringing an icy rain that turned to hail. Those wearing shorts and t-shirts wondered aloud where summer had gone. Gusting wind took over from gravity, and the hail, chased by waves of water, came at us sideways. The transition from sweating to incipient hypothermia lasted a matter of minutes.

Later, shielded from the wind and with a dry sweater on, I reflected on what an interaction with the real world entails. First, it is about paying attention to your surroundings and the weather. In many respects it is being aware that we are indeed small, insignificant and vulnerable. From that flows an appreciation for the topography and the forces that sculpted and moulded the landscape. At various scales, the timelines are cosmic, geological and biological. We are at the tail end of the latter one.

It is also about associations – the cow parsnip patch in the avalanche slope is a pasture for grizzlies. The huckleberry patch isn't just a sweet treat – it is a triumph of botany over frost, aided by pollinators and enough accumulated heat units from the sun. Mariposa lily, Indian paintbrush and fireweed tell a story of niches, needs, relationships and season. Beauty, in the natural world and maybe elsewhere too, lies in the details. The tapestry that is the landscape is a weave of stories, some evident, others less so. Mostly, though, it is about humility and respect.

In another valley, not so far away, the sound of running water, birdsong and wind was interrupted on a regular basis with motor noise from off-highway vehicles (OHV). As I watched a crowd of quad enthusiasts manoeuvre up a rutted, rough trail I realized these people can't afford to be distracted drivers. Each was fixated with eyes on the ground a few feet ahead of their front tires. Not only do they not notice me, they also miss or are oblivious to the wildflowers, the downy woodpecker, a phalanx of ravens and likely the aroma of warm pine forest.

If driving an OHV is a family-oriented sport and it gets people outdoors, how does it influence them to appreciate, have some empathy for the natural environment, instead of using the landscape as a natural racetrack and enduro course?

I doubt the stories they will tell around the campfire, outside of their elaborate recreational vehicles, will dwell on the natural world. More likely they will be about equipment, miles of trails traversed, mudholes stuck in and the travesty of closing trails to OHV use.

I'm guessing, of course, about their conversations. However, it does seem to me that people engaged in activities detached from landscape appreciation, like mountain biking, downhill skiing, white-water rafting, trail running, riding the zip line and OHV activity, among others, are a rapidly increasing segment of users of wild country.

I get the sense these users probably view the wild setting as a backdrop but perhaps with little connection or engagement. Wild places are used in the same way that physical fitness aficionados change the video for their stationary bicycles at the gym. Though numbers of wild country users may be impressive, what they might gain in terms of understanding, connection or empathy might still be marginal.

Probably the motivations include the adrenalin rushes of challenge, competition and thrill seeking. What they don't include is insight and contemplation of the landscape. I would guess we would have some spirited discussions about different interpretations of mindfulness. The most critical aspect missing is humility, the recognition that wild places don't care about us, our safety or our ambitions.

Georgia O'Keeffe, the landscape painter, wisely said, "Nobody sees a flower really; it is so small. We haven't time, and to see takes time – like a friend takes time." When we treat wild places as a treadmill or a carnival ride, we miss the small moments of natural beauty, the ecosystem functions they represent and the connections to us. It is a dichotomy, maybe a chasm, between those who see utility, beauty and purpose in the entire wild landscape and those who see (or use) it as a racetrack, parking lot or a thrill palace.

The pleasure, perhaps the necessity, of self-propelled travel through wild areas is to free oneself from the encumbrances that civilization imposes – the distractions of noise, complexity, artificial light and control.

"The smaller we come to feel ourselves compared to the mountain, the nearer we come to participating in its goodness" said Arne Naess, the originator of the concept of "deep ecology." The problem with scaling the metaphorical mountain in a 4×4, or on an OHV or riding a chairlift, is that it is less likely we can participate in the goodness that wild places provide us.

Under your own power, in a wild place, you experience real time, real space, floating at nature's pace, and are unencumbered by gasoline engines, battery-powered devices and other artifacts of modern design. You learn space can only be measured by the time and energy (and sweat) it takes to walk across it, instead of the technological illusion of space and time shrinking. Under steam from some other energy source than our own, there is the obliteration of real time and space – no wonder we sense a disconnect.

Activities like walking, swimming, paddling and cross-country skiing create a state where the mind, the body and the world align themselves together, like a musical chord. Every other conveyance isolates us from the environment, blocks us from essential sights, sounds, smells and sensations.

Slow-paced, human-powered transport is leisurely enough to be able to experience these sensations, to absorb them and add them to our memory bank. We are connected – foot to earth, paddle to water and ski to snow. The mind, like our feet, works best at speeds not exceeding five kilometres an hour.

When you walk your soul feels like part of the landscape. It is the pace, the measured pace of foot travel, that slows us down mentally, allowing a connection to the land being travelled on. Walking is a sensual engagement with terrain, weather, wildlife and one's own thoughts. Nature seeps into you. It's probably good for us both physically and psychologically. When we concentrate on breathing, benefits occur, like loosening the tyranny of trivial things. I forget the other benefits.

Bruce Chatwin, explorer and writer, told the following story to make the point about travel speed: "A white explorer in Africa, anxious to press ahead with his journey paid his porters for a series of forced marches. But they, almost within reach of their destination, set down their bundles and refused to budge. No amount of extra payment would convince them otherwise. They said they had to wait for their souls to catch up."

Our souls need to catch up, to allow the slow absorption of beauty. This cannot be hurried. We need to move slowly, under our own power in these places where we ask the land what its evolving story is, where we align ourselves with its primordial energies, places to walk our talk and where we place and can feel the soles of our feet on the soul of the world.

Wild places aren't necessarily quiet, but human noise is missing. Debbie Webster, a bed and breakfast operator on the east flank of the Livingstone Range, poses the question for her clients to ponder: "How loud can quiet be?" You must listen for it, and then you can hear it. It has a strange, beautiful texture. It has a quality and a dimension all its own. As the subtlety in Debbie's message implies, you can listen to silence and learn from it.

Aldo Leopold observed that quiet, wild country is hard to find since "mechanized recreation already has seized nine-tenths of the woods and mountains; a decent respect for minorities should declare the other tenth to wilderness."

Where can wild country be found, according to Douglas Chadwick, is largely in parks and protected areas. He calls them the "gold standard" of natural laboratories, "listening posts" where one can hear what nature has to say without human interruption and human footprint. These places are harder to find than most people think or suspect.

Charles Lacy, the late biologist and artist, said, based on his reflection on changes in Alberta, "It is becoming increasingly difficult to experience the beauty, peace and solitude that only wild lands can provide. Many will never have the opportunity. I hope that my art can preserve for others these things that have given me so much pleasure and can also help save them from further depletion." We have lost our sense of "awe" and need wild places to reinfect ourselves.

Aldo Leopold, in 1935, observed the unintended consequences of development on his country: "This country has been swinging the hammer of development so long and so hard it has forgotten the anvil of wilderness which gave value and significance to its labors. The momentum of our blows is so unprecedented that the remaining remnant of wilderness will be pounded into road-dust before we find out its values." The sentiment could also apply to Alberta, where road-dust from too many roads and noise from mechanized recreation wears away at the soul of those in search of tranquil wild places.

The wild is a place to experience joy and fear, sometimes almost simultaneously, is expansive enough to require effort to explore it (and maybe get lost there), where the sounds are of nature and the silence is deafening. As Annick Smith explores in her short story "Huckleberries," "One reason we go into the wild is to escape to a place where elements are basic, and it is necessary to notice them."

What do wild places mean? The opportunity to see a grizzly rise majestically from a huckleberry patch; fording a chilling stream as a native cutthroat trout rises to a stonefly hatch; seeing the horizon disappear over a grassland so appealing you'd like to roll in it; hearing the warblers return to a piece of the boreal forest so large you shrink in size, humbled by the scale; and feeling the lash of the rain followed by the drying power of the sun.

We need these places more than we can know, we need more of these places than we can envision, and we need to move more quickly to protect those places still left.

*Illustration by Liz Saunders*

# 9
# Noah, You Missed the Fish

*Fish are as easy to count as trees —*
*except they're invisible and they move.*

—John Shepherd

## A TROUT IS A TROUT IS A TROUT, ISN'T IT?

———

Amid snobbish trout anglers there are clear preferences, although under pressure some might admit all trout are equal, but some are more equal than others. My friend, who can catch fish in a ditch, and sometimes does when the irrigation canals are running, contends a trout is a trout is a trout. Well, isn't it? He shares this sentiment with a majority of anglers, some fish managers, senior bureaucrats and the general public. Among the public, the link to wild fish is limited to fish sticks or what comes out of a can.

Where does this attitude leave our precarious populations of native trout, especially the westslope cutthroat trout, besieged as it is by habitat issues and hybridization with non-native rainbow trout?

The late Robert Behnke, professor of fishery and wildlife biology at Colorado State University and an acknowledged expert on salmonid fishes, observed, "the present diversity of western trout evolved in response to different selective factors operating in different geographic regions."

Within the trout and salmon "family" specializations are apparent, and within these are further adaptations that have fine-tuned life histories to favour survival in relation to local climates, variability in stream flows, water temperature fluctuations, fire, flood and drought events, predators and co-existing fish species. For our native cutthroat trout, their specialty has become the headwater streams of the Oldman and Bow watersheds.

Stepping back in time about 40 to 50 million years ago, we see that the wild fish we now know as the trout and salmon, the graylings, and the whitefish had separated into unique families, diverging from some earlier ancestral line. About 30 to 40 million years ago the trout and salmon group divided again, one branch leading to include bull trout and brook trout (sometimes referred to as "charrs"), the other to incorporate the salmon and other trout.

The branch called *Oncorhynchus* includes the Pacific salmon and western trout. The genus name comes from the Greek "hooked nose," referring to the hooked jaws of males during spawning. Rainbow trout and cutthroat trout diverged from a common ancestor perhaps two to three million years ago, according to Dr. Behnke. This provides a sense of the antiquity of our native trout, and the time they have spent adjusting to the conditions of a turbulent world.

We probably can't imagine how turbulent a world it was as our trout figured out how to make a living. This was the Pleistocene Epoch, which stretched from about three million years before present to about 12,000 years ago, last Tuesday. This was a colder, drier period with maybe as many as 20 alternating cycles of glacial advance and retreat.

In the last advance, imagine ice towering two kilometres over the Calgary Tower. Ice blockages and ice dams changed flow patterns for major drainages, fortuitously allowing several of our native trout species to cross the continental divide, eastward. The ice dams periodically broke, sending successive waves of destructive force across the landscape. To survive, trout found glacial refuges.

In the succeeding epoch, as cutthroat trout moved into the "new" watersheds of what would become Alberta, they dealt with periodic flooding, of magnitudes unimaginable by today's standards. Then there was the "mega-drought" of the late 16th century and other prolonged drought periods that make droughts of the 1930s and 1980s appear as wet periods. Volcanoes erupted, most notably Mount Mazama, but also others, layering the landscape with a thick ash layer. The range of variability trout dealt with, when measured over long periods of time, shows us a sombre reflection of their staying power.

How did native trout like the cutthroat manage this feat? Evolution isn't a random process. The genetic variation on which natural selection acts may occur randomly, but natural selection isn't random at all. The survival and reproductive success of cutthroat trout is directly related to the ways its inherited traits function in the context of the watersheds of the Oldman and Bow.

Genetic variants that survived and reproduced were much more likely to succeed than ones that didn't. Variation, it is said, was "the coal that fed Darwin's locomotive of natural selection." Natural selection favours mutations that provide some sort of advantage. For example, over time the sleek profile of a trout, which allows them manoeuvrability and less energy expenditure in fast-flowing water, has been selected over the blocky profile of a walleye.

Similar "designs" have resulted, as in rainbow trout and cutthroat trout, from a common ancestor, but both evolved in different situations. This does not necessarily mean that one can effectively replace the other. Different selective pressures result in very different ecological adaptations.

We humans are a study in genetic adaptation. Initially our body form was a response to climate. From tropical regions, body form was tall and lean to better dissipate heat. In polar and alpine regions, heat conservation was key so body forms were short and stout. However, cultural adaptations have allowed us to populate most of the world, irrespective of our genetic origins. Cutthroat trout have no similar cultural adaptations, like clothing, central heating and agriculture. Their survival turns on their ability to adapt to the conditions offered.

Dr. Behnke's research indicates rainbow trout evolved in the Columbia River watershed and have been restricted geographically from westslope cutthroat trout for a long time, suggesting the ancestors of the two species evolved in isolation from each other. Because of this, cutthroat lack the innate isolating mechanisms (like separate spawning times, places and behaviours) that might allow them to coexist with non-native trout species, especially rainbows. That's why hybridization occurs between the species when rainbow trout are stocked into native cut-throat waters.

Unprotected sex between rainbow and cutthroats has not formed a genetic conga line of hearty robustness – the hybrid vigour theory – but instead one of dilution of some of the essential traits. Hybridization brings a breakdown in some of the locally adapted cutthroat traits, which diminishes survival of the crosses. Cutthroat trout with as little as 20 per cent of rainbow genetics are only half as reproductively successful.

The Athabasca rainbow trout (Alberta's only native rainbow trout) may have had its origins in the Fraser River system. Ironically, in one watershed of the Athabasca system this species is threatened by hybridization from a stocking of cutthroat trout.

The rainbow trout has been extensively used in fish culture operations and spread widely, not just in North America but around the world. Once a population of rainbow trout has been domesticated by rigorous selection to perform well under hatchery conditions, especially favouring traits of tractability, growth and survival under artificial conditions, the genetic changes become detriments to survival under natural conditions of harshness and variability.

On the surface, or perhaps below the waters' surface, rainbow trout seem to have carved out a substantial niche in Alberta waters. The famous fisheries of the Bow and Crowsnest rivers are formed on the fins of the species. These waters were, in living history, the realm of the cutthroat and the bull trout. Now, with habitat deterioration coupled with a past aggressive campaign of stocking hatchery rainbows, these rivers and many other smaller streams are no longer cutthroat waters.

The rainbow trout fisheries of the Bow and Oldman might give the impression that native trout stocks are replaceable, that protecting the genetic diversity they represent is anachronistic, and a trout is a trout is a trout. Cutthroat trout have committed to the long haul, the extended view, and so should we as ultimate arbiters of their existence.

Bison and domestic cows are related species, belonging to the same family, and serve to illustrate the fundamental differences between them just as rainbow and cutthroat trout are different despite familial ties. The evolutionary histories of cows and bison demonstrate significant differences in pressures that translate into strikingly different modes of resource use.

Bison adapted to survive winters on the plains of North America, even the deep snows of Yellowstone National Park. Alternately, the domestic cow hangs around water, doesn't migrate to more amenable conditions and handily dies during severe winters without supplemental feeding and shelter. So a cow isn't just a domesticated bison and is not a replacement for one.

A rainbow trout isn't a cutthroat trout and vice versa. That's not to suggest the rainbow hasn't evolved to fit the watersheds of its origins, but those origins were not the streams of the southern Eastern Slopes.

The stocking of rainbow trout (and other non-native species) was based on a perception that angling pressure had significantly reduced trout populations and streams needed "seeding" to supplement wild stocks. Fisheries science had not progressed far enough to understand the innate capability of wild fish to self-replenish if angling pressure was moderated. Wild populations of cutthroat were initially tapped to supplement streams, but again, the perception was that native fish weren't up to the task, compared with the more abundant stocks of rainbow trout flowing out of early fish hatcheries.

As settlement progressed, driven by people from other areas with inherent allegiances to other fish species, our native fish were deemed less "sporting," based on unfamiliarity, perceptions of poorer angling quality, and a typical frontier tendency not to value native species. Overriding this was a failure to grasp the long adaptive tenure of cutthroat trout with streams of the southern Eastern Slopes.

While early rainbow trout stocking began not long after the turn of the 20th century, streams along the foothills were subjected to intensive stocking programs from the 1930s through the 1960s, with the construction of the Forestry Trunk Road being a driver of stocking farther westward. That means non-native rainbow trout have a history of about 25 generations in Alberta. By comparison, native cutthroat have invested over 4,000 generations in adaptation to our southern watersheds. They are the ones that have rolled the storms, the variability and the uncertainty into their genetic material, not their distant cousin, a recent interloper.

Wild, native and genetically pure westslope cutthroat trout and their habitats are as far as you can get from Disneyland – the artificial, contrived and plastic theme park. Cutthroat trout are genuine, with no artificial colour or flavour added.

They were the trout of Kootenai Brown, the spark plug for establishment of Waterton Lakes National Park. They were the trout of Bert Riggall and Andy Russell, early guides, outfitters and conservationists in the Oldman watershed. They were the trout of Jimmy Simpson, an early resident and entrepreneur in Banff National Park. And they were the species of choice for

Dr. R.B. Miller, Alberta's first fisheries biologist, who started down a long road of gaining appreciation for cutthroat trout and studying the madness of imposing non-native rainbows on top of them.

So, a trout is not a trout, is not a trout, and is not a trout, based on genetics, adaptation and survival.

## HUNTING FOR THE LAST GOLDEYE

The quintessential river of Alberta's parkland is the Battle. It begins in Battle Lake, west of Wetaskiwin. A lazy river, it seems in no hurry to meet the North Saskatchewan River near Battleford in Saskatchewan. The Battle cannot depend on snow accumulation from high-elevation forests to sustain flows. Instead, 144 big and little tributaries provide the lifeblood of the river – the groundwater, springs, seeps and runoff. Most of these streams are unnamed and start in someone's backyard.

Anthony Henday, possibly the first European to explore what would become Alberta, travelled up the Battle River in 1754 with a band of Cree. His journals report that on the occasion of his first camp in the watershed, probably near the present Alberta–Saskatchewan border, they caught 17 small "trout" in one creek of running water. Henday was from Britain and presumably would have recognized trout. Unfortunately, his route is difficult to put into modern context, so the location of this stream with trout is a mystery.

John Palliser crossed Pigeon Lake Creek, one of the Battle River's larger tributaries, in October 1858 travelling to Fort

Edmonton. He recounted, "They had to swim Pigeon Creek, which was deep, though it was only 20 feet wide." One would be hard pressed to wade the creek now in October and do much more than wet one's feet. Yet the histories of early settlement of the Battle watershed are replete with stories of catching fish, lots of fish and big fish, in the river and its tributaries, with traps, nets and spears.

Goldeye have a prominent place in the fishing stories from the past. Goldeye are deep-bodied fish, flattened laterally and silvery with large scales. They are named for their large, yellow-gold eyes, which are adapted to vision in dim light and turbid water.

The goldeye, when smoked, was considered one of the finest of all eating fish and figured prominently on the menus in the dining cars of the CPR. Then they were known as "Winnipeg goldeye" because of the original source in Lake Winnipeg. In an old bulletin of the Fisheries Research Board of Canada two biologists, Kennedy and Sprules, described the fish in the following way:

> A "Winnipeg goldeye" represents the triumph of art over
> nature. Its characteristic color results from an aniline dye.
> Its characteristic taste is essentially that of oak wood
> smoke. Its texture has been improved by freezing.
> Its name is derived from a lake where it is no longer
> caught in appreciable quantities.

The goldeye of the Battle River were as tasty as those caught farther east in Lake Winnipeg. Harley Louis of the Montana First Nation near Maskwacis recalled fish traps in the 1940s: "We'd catch enough fish [goldeye] to fill our saddlebags and ride back for a big feed of fish with our families."

But, as is the case with the bounty of new countries, it did not last.

By 1977, when Dave Christiansen, a provincial fisheries biologist, floated the river he was told the big runs of goldeye were nearly gone and goldeye could only be caught near the lower end of the Battle River. Fishing was "so much better in the past," said local residents. Other fish like northern pike were also suffering from low oxygen levels in the river, which contributed to massive fish die-offs. Dave recalls the Battle River was a stagnant stream by late summer. The Battle River was, he said, "A river on the ropes going through its death throes."

Just as the goldeye population of Lake Winnipeg crashed, probably from overharvest, the goldeye of the Battle River have crashed for a variety of reasons, probably the triumph of development over nature.

A fish biodiversity study of 128 kilometres of the river, in sections from the headwaters at Battle Lake to the border and undertaken between 2005 and 2007, captured just seven goldeye. A few pike and walleye were found, but 80 per cent of the catch consisted of white suckers and minnows. Suckers are tough, resilient fish capable of survival in reduced circumstances. Even they were suffering lesions, eroded fins and growths.

A provincial government river monitoring program found that over the span of 2009 to 2010 the Battle River had the lowest water quality of all river sites monitored in Alberta.

What's the matter with the Battle River?

Dr. Michael Sullivan, Provincial Fish Science Specialist, sums it up succinctly with, "too many nutrients coupled with too few filters spells big trouble for fish."

Phosphorus is a nutrient and is the building block for plant growth. Amounts in excess of what plants require tend to wash into the river, where the addition has the same effect on algal growth. One unit of phosphorus derived from animal manure or synthetic fertilizer can exponentially grow 500 units of algae. Over winter the die-off and decomposition of algae consumes oxygen, lowering dissolved oxygen concentrations to lethal levels for fish.

In February and March 2010, the concentration of dissolved oxygen in the Battle River under ice cover was measured throughout its length. For over half the river's length there was not enough dissolved oxygen present to support most fish species. Excessive nutrients stimulate both growth and death.

What has changed from yesterday's Battle River to the one of today?

The water retention capability of the watershed has been drastically compromised. Less than 2 per cent of the watershed is now wooded, and approximately 75 per cent of the wetlands, the essential sponge and moderating influence for flow, are now missing. Many of the places referenced in historical accounts no longer contain fish or, in many cases, even water.

The early wave of pioneers into Central Alberta were attracted by a combination of good soil, water, wood for building and abundant fish and wildlife populations. They farmed with horses and steam equipment. This limited capability did not result in significant changes to the landscape.

After the Second World War and into the 1950s, the countryside changed dramatically. Demand for feed grain for livestock increased at the same time that bridges and better roads provided access to more grain elevators. Higher farm profits sparked more mechanization with greater tractor horsepower and bigger tillage equipment. The availability of huge bulldozers of sufficient size to shear and pile aspen forests created larger fields. The use of synthetic fertilizers to boost crop production and the availability of herbicides and pesticides to combat crop diseases and pests began in the 1950s.

As the wave of settlement and development spread and the ecological integrity of the watershed became more and more compromised, fish numbers, distribution and health all declined. Profound shifts in water quality, especially nutrients from our activities, followed clearing of the forests, drainage of wetlands, more cultivated acreage, more livestock and fewer natural riparian filters and buffers.

It wasn't the space race, nor the arms race, but the food production race, aided by the horsepower race in farming that led to the decline and disappearance of native fish from watercourses in the settled portion of Alberta.

Curiously, there is safe haven for fish in the Battle River within the boundaries of CFB Wainwright, a military base. This isn't a function of armed soldiers protecting fish, but rather a landscape that is relatively unchanged since the time of Henday.

The military base, formerly Buffalo National Park, is uncultivated, uncleared native aspen parkland. Wetlands and tributaries within the base are intact, and as a result nutrient loading to the river is closer to the range of natural variation. The absorptive capacity of the landscape also means springs and seeps provide a consistent supply of groundwater to the river. Riparian areas are intact and well vegetated.

The Battle River through the military base is where the last few goldeye can find habitat conditions to their liking. It's also where pike and walleye populations make their last stand. The lesson from this safe haven on the Battle River is that effective fish population maintenance and restoration is based on habitat. Everything else done on behalf of fish pales beside watershed integrity and is mostly feel-good, cosmetic window dressing.

Even a goldeye can see that.

## IN THE BEDROOMS OF THE BULL TROUT

The tug upstream seems inexorable, an urge not to be denied or ignored. Up bull trout swim, from the wide expanses of river, from the comparative security of deep pools and boulder-choked riffles. Upstream, against a rapidly increasing current, in a channel that narrows and gets shallower. Upstream, where water temperatures drop perceptibly, and the medium becomes so clear fish appear to be suspended rather than immersed.

Streamlined and torpedo-shaped, bull trout move in a timeless migration. Their destinations are the spots where each emerged from the stream gravels some five to ten years earlier. Each survivor has bulked up substantially. Nothing escapes them – suckers, mountain whitefish, big stoneflies and the occasional mouse, vole and snake. To get big you must eat big.

Bull trout are the ultimate aquatic predator, at the top of the watery food chain. Think of them as scaled grizzlies, with gills. Nowadays a big one might top out at four kilograms. In earlier days, remembered still by elderly anglers, a big one might stretch over a saddle and dangle nearly from stirrup to stirrup. In the waters of their spawning tributaries these giants would only be partially submerged.

Their movements upstream are anything but random. The magnet that pulls, attracts them, is the unique combination of cool groundwater bubbling up from some subterranean reservoir through gravels shaped from the persistent grinding action of erosion. Context here is everything. It takes a watershed, not just a stream, to meet bull trout needs for the biological imperative of replacing themselves.

Forests, generally of the intact, mature variety, with thick underlays of absorbent mosses capture and store snowmelt and rainfall. This water, the unheralded treasure of forests, slowly is entrained below the surface. There it is then meted out just as slowly to add to streamflow. That these streams flow in the winter when all else seems frozen is the magic of this unseen supply of water. Bull trout appreciate it more than we seem to, for their eggs are deposited in the gravels in the fall and survival is dependent on this interplay between surface and groundwater.

The seeps and springs are not often obvious to our eyes. What was obvious to early hunters, trappers and anglers was the autumn splashing of female trout absorbed in moving gravels. Around them, like teenagers at a high school dance, the males vied with each other for position. Often these fish were of such a size that the shallow riffles couldn't provide enough depth. Heads, fins and backs would protrude into the alien environment of air. To be successful in the dance of sex requires bull trout to comprehend the nuances of water movement, depth, velocity and changes during the winter of egg incubation. The combination must be one of hydrological experience and clairvoyance.

I get to play fisheries biologist again, for a few days, on one of the ongoing inventories of bull trout in the upper Oldman watershed. On a late and crisp September day I accompany Matthew Coombs, then the only fisheries biologist for southwestern Alberta. On paper Matthew has a small area in which to ply his trade – just the entire headwaters of the Oldman watershed from the US border to the boundary with the Bow watershed. It reminds me, painfully, of the minimal priority placed on fish by the province of Alberta.

Dutch Creek is a tributary to the Oldman River. The stories of big bull trout, and many of them from the dusty archives stored in the memories of elderly anglers, are hard to square with today's reality. Less than one out of ten bull trout now chooses Dutch Creek as a spawning destination. Dutch Creek (and its near twin, Racehorse Creek) are watersheds checkerboarded with logging clear-cuts. A little cyber-trip on Google Earth shows the footprint of logging in these watersheds to be extensive.

We slip on our chest waders to count bull trout redds in a reach of Dutch Creek. Matthew warns me the water is very cold. Fresh snow ices the peaks of the continental divide and frost coats the ground. None of this registers until my feet desert me on the slick boulders and I stick an arm in the water to steady myself. The water is numbingly cold. As I wring out my shirt sleeve, I marvel at creatures that make this glacial medium their home.

Redds are the "nests" bull trout mothers excavate in the gravels. First on their minds is the selection of an appropriate spot, an inscrutable science to we who live in air, not water. What seems evident is that the female must sense the presence of an intergravular flow of water. That flow is crucial to provide oxygenated water to the incubating eggs and to flush away metabolic wastes. Additionally, that flow must persist throughout the overwinter incubation period until the eggs hatch in the spring. This explains why groundwater is so key to bull trout.

If the water-witching is successful, the female then turns on her side and with a vigorous wave-like undulation of her body and tail uses a hydraulic shock wave of water to dislodge stream bed gravels and cobbles. This blast of water flushes away sediment and creates a depression. Into this depression she lays some of her eggs, attended to by a randy male who completes the conjugal unit. The process is repeated, moving upstream, covering the previous excavation and creating a new one for more eggs.

Over the course of this the female will move several times her own weight of gravels and cobbles. Counting these redds provides an indication of population size. Monitoring year to year helps gauge population trends.

This is one of those clear, bright blue days of extended summer. Snow-capped peaks give evidence the summer season is ending, but the day tells the lie that it will persist. Dutch Creek is clearing; a rainstorm the previous day clouded the water with sediment. What happens in the uplands of a watershed inevitably follows the fundamentals of gravity. The footprint of disturbed land, the clear-cuts, roads and trails, continues to bleed sediment, and even a slight rainstorm mobilizes that sediment.

We walk upstream in the channel, looking for the telltale signs of redds – oval signatures of stream gravels cleansed of their patina of algae and silt. On reach after reach, I mentally challenge myself to discern the signs that would indicate a bull trout would find the place pleasing. So many of the reaches seem to have the right stuff – suitable water depth, sufficient velocity, appropriately sized substrate and overhead cover. But we find few redds.

Stymied, we consider the reasons for trout rejection. The gravel holds a clue. It is solid under our feet, and when we probe it with our measuring sticks it yields only to excessive force. Despite the appearance of being clean, it takes a human-scaled effort to excavate a depression. This is not the usual loose, friable substrate where a step leaves a footprint behind. Alarmingly, this is pavement, aggregate cemented together with sediment giving an outward appearance of a roughed surface. Without pickaxe or jackhammer no trout could penetrate this stuff.

The count for a six-kilometre wade is a disappointing ten redds. In Hidden Creek, another Oldman River tributary, nearly ten times as many redds have been counted in a four-kilometre stretch. None of this is surprising when one connects the dots between land use and fish populations.

Logging, the predominant land use, has a greater impact on streams than on forests because of the long-term nature of effects in and on streams. A subtle and less evident change is in runoff – both the amount and the speed of delivery. For a species like bull trout that are reliant on groundwater, subtle shifts in hydrologic response from forest harvest is a problem.

The connection between logging and streams is less subtle when roads are considered. The scientific literature abounds with information on the effects of logging and associated roading on trout populations. Roads funnel, streamline and contribute to sediment delivery. Wherever studied, the impacts are real, measurable, long-term and negative.

A clear conclusion, across the research, is that as road densities (and the number of stream crossings) increase, the proportion of streams that support strong, healthy populations of trout diminish. All aquatic species have adapted to periodic disturbance, but roading increases sediment delivery, sometimes by an order of magnitude greater than the natural background levels. But sediment delivery is just the tip of the problem.

Decades of research in experimental watersheds shows only a fraction of the sediment eroded will work its way downstream, out of the stream system. Measurement in the usual short monitoring period consistently underestimates sediment yield from land use. Much of it is stored in the stream bed and within the substrate. Researchers term the residence time for that sediment as "centennial" time. There it lingers, migrating downstream as little as a few metres a year to perhaps a kilometre a year in larger rivers. Mike Miles, a fluvial geomorphologist, calls it "a slow-moving train of sediment."

Recent research in nearby streams in the Oldman watershed confirms these impacts. Comparing undisturbed with disturbed (i.e., logged) watersheds clearly shows substantial increases in sediment even after logging ceases. Most alarming is the amount of sediment from logging and roading entrained in the substrate. From paired watersheds, logged systems have 2.5 times more entrained sediment.

The impacts are neither fleeting nor transitory. As the sediment settles in for the long haul, it reduces the depth and quality of pools. Less evident is the infilling of the interstitial spaces between the gravels, where trout eggs incubate and insects (the building blocks of fish flesh) live. As it infiltrates the gaps, some of the sediment bonds, effectively cementing together the substrate materials.

This cemented layer, which may extend down some distance into the substrate, becomes resistant to periodic flushing flows. Reduced permeability of the substrate, the ability of water to percolate up or down, becomes another impact on bull trout. Like tar in a smoker's lungs, the accumulated sediment squeezes the life out of streams. So, even as the forest may regenerate, the legacy of logging will persist as an influence on streams and all the aquatic creatures over centennial time.

We may have inadvertently doomed trout populations in logged watersheds to a slow, drawn-out and anticlimactic end, like a candle finally burning out. In the Oldman River, watershed bull trout are missing from 70 per cent of their former range.

The overwhelming and unfortunate legacy of land-use decisions and their cumulative effects will haunt these watersheds until the last native fish slips away and all that remain are ghosts. Without an ecosystem approach and more balance in decisions about land use, soon we might be arguing over the last bull trout. By then it will be too late. Watersheds with an extensive logging footprint need quick remedial actions and mitigation involving road closures and rehabilitation if native fish are to be saved.

We should be using bull trout as an indicator, an icon of the health and integrity of our headwaters. Their continued presence and increasing abundance would provide a strong signal that we know how to manage these vital watersheds. And, to many of us who see bull trout (and all native species) in that context, it is about a sense of place, centuries old.

Bull trout know place, know how to return home, and they know where they came from. All they require of us is to acknowledge their presence and needs as well as share the watershed with them in ways that don't contribute to them winking out of existence.

Sadly, our industrial focus for the Forest Reserve is not far removed from the pursuit of buffalo hides and tongues. The resource economy of logging is equally simplistic, rapacious and blind. It would appear the decline of bull trout provincially and in the Oldman watershed has slipped beneath the consciousness and conscience of the land manager, the Forest Service. In the words of David Brower, founder of the Sierra Club, it is as if "the relationship of everything to everything else and how it is not working is so comprehensive no one can comprehend it."

Splashing up Dutch Creek puts into sharp focus that neither the Forest Service nor the timber industry has yet demonstrated the soft, sensitive, careful touch required to maintain bull trout habitat and to keep sediment from streams.

The cost of repetitive logging mistakes in sensitive watersheds is too high to continue ignoring the problem of industrial-scale timber harvest. Pierre Trudeau, long the bogeyman for Alberta, once famously said, "The state has no business in the bedrooms of the nation." To paraphrase that, logging has no business in the bedrooms of the bull trout.

## FIXING A BROKEN SPECIES
### *Challenges in the Recovery of Westslope Cutthroat Trout*

———

My grandfather's pocket watch lies heavy in my palm. On the back, arrayed against the silver of the case, is an embossed golden horseshoe. That horseshoe, slightly raised, is worn nearly through, maybe like the luck it used to imply. Time and luck have run out for the watch, since it is broken and no longer repairable.

As with my grandfather's watch, time has run out for some westslope cutthroat trout populations and is rapidly running out for others. Threatened is the current term used to express their status in Alberta. Maybe "extinguished" would be appropriate for some streams.

Cutthroat trout are now absent from 94 per cent of their historic range. Once there were more cutthroat trout than people in Alberta; now we vastly outnumber the remaining genetically pure trout. There is a very low bench strength for recovery of cutthroat populations.

Recovery goals, provincially and federally, include protecting and expanding the current range of genetically pure populations. *Pure* is defined as a percentage of genetic material that is true to type, greater or equal to 99 per cent. In other words, the real, unadulterated trout, not mixed with non-native rainbow trout genes. Hybridization with rainbow trout is a particularly vexing problem.

The evolutionary fate of hybridized populations is unknown as yet, because it is a paradox. Genetic mixing is believed to reduce fitness, yet despite that hybridization has progressed rapidly.

Dr. Michael Sullivan, the provincial fish science specialist, describes the three horsemen of fisheries apocalypse as "harvest, habitat and hybridization." Cutthroat trout were easy to catch – too easy. Their declines led to the thought that stocking was necessary, and non-native rainbow trout and other trout species were poured into cutthroat waters. Successive waves of industrial, agricultural and recreational land uses have washed over most of the watersheds containing cutthroat trout. The number of intact watersheds – mostly unroaded, unlogged and undeveloped – have shrunk like ice cubes on a hot stove.

Against this backdrop, provincial fisheries biologists, national parks biologists, conservation groups and independent biologists are working together on a quest to fix a broken species.

The first major challenge was an inventory of cutthroat trout populations, with genetic analysis to determine the degree of purity. This was no small task, and information on overlooked populations is still trickling in. Like stock-taking in a store, the inventory of cutthroat trout provided the information to determine status, a prelude to listing it as a species at risk. This is also crucial to development of a recovery strategy. Locations where cutthroat are found currently are vastly overwhelmed by those where they are now missing. That alone should provide a sense of urgency for recovery.

If that task wasn't daunting enough, the next steps for recovery make the work of the basic inventory pale by comparison. It will be critically important to grow the pure population of cutthroat, in as many places as feasible, as quickly as possible, while ensuring existing populations are protected from peril.

So how does one grow a fish population? Unfortunately, there is no cutthroat trout store available to get more. Range expansion is possible when pure trout are moved into a few barren waters upstream of waterfalls. This is population insurance but does not meet a full recovery goal. A primary recovery goal is to return them to much of their previous range, where many streams are now occupied with hybridized trout.

To repopulate those streams requires an abundant supply of pure cutthroat trout, and the strategy involves the development of a hatchery brood stock. As David Mayhood, a fisheries researcher with considerable experience with the species, points out, "Westslope cutthroat trout have developed many unique evolutionary nuances throughout their range." This constitutes a resource of genetic and life history diversity.

Creating a brood stock has to respect this feature of the species, as Andreas Luek, a senior fisheries biologist, explained. The inventory of cutthroat waters provided a place to start. The upper Oldman River watershed had connected populations and the best opportunities to tap for brood stock development. Find some spawning cutthroat trout, capture them, strip and fertilize the eggs, and presto – a brood stock in the making. If only it were that simple.

Cutthroat trout are spring spawners – a time of snowmelt, rainfall, flooding and often turbid water conditions. Knowing trout are present in a stream is one thing. Finding them in a narrow window of time while they are spawning is another. If a needle in a haystack is a challenge to find, imagine the situation faced by fishery biologists with cutthroat trout.

Trout populations in tiny tributaries of the upper Oldman River are small, and it is unwise to remove too much of the reproductive potential. One can't rob Peter to pay Paul, so trout eggs from a number of tributaries are amalgamated into the formation of a "composite" brood stock. This required additional genetic testing to determine if all were of pure derivation, ensuring the various populations to be mixed were connected, sharing similar traits and the individuals were disease free.

A coordinated effort, spread over several seasons, required up to 12 teams to locate trout, capture them and secure their eggs. This will continue for several more years until a large enough brood stock is assembled for eventual return to streams.

Return of the progeny of brood stock to streams will be done with a technique called remote site incubation, or RSI. The eggs of pure cutthroat trout, from the wild or brood stock, are allowed to eye up (indicating they have been fertilized) in a hatchery facility and then are placed into instream RSI units to hatch. The fry then swim out of the units into the stream.

As Brian Meagher, the provincial fisheries biologist who has evaluated the technique, says, "This gives these trout an almost immediate head start in the stream where they will spend their lives." The technique seems to provide a substantial improvement in survival over nature, almost quadrupling the number of trout that will swim into a new life.

The next steps, like where to put the progeny of the brood stock, have yet to be worked out, but are the most critical in terms of recovery goals. Multiple, overlapping and sometimes opposing issues arise. Given these challenges, it would be good to take a moment to appreciate the task fisheries biologists have in recovery efforts for cutthroat trout.

Challenges in population restoration include determining what is the critical population size to be able to survive upsets and persist over the long term. Is there capacity in the hatchery for brood stock and for quarantining eggs? The RSI techniques will need to be scaled up to match population recovery goals.

Then will come the thorny question, How to deal with hybridized populations? Can they be swamped with pure-strain fish and slowly improve the genetics? Will some systems require the removal of hybrids before the stocking of pure trout occurs? How will this be achieved? Will it require the use of rotenone, a fish poison, or can it be done with electrofishing? What will be the public receptivity to the use of rotenone, and what engagement will be required with stakeholders?

Where it will be impossible to completely remove hybrids, can barriers to upstream movement be installed, to separate populations? What is the overlap with bull trout populations (also Threatened) and recovery actions for that species? How will other species like mountain whitefish be affected?

How will anglers react to temporary losses of angling opportunity and what angling regulations will be required to protect pure populations? How can public and political support be maintained over the long period of time required for recovery efforts?

Habitat restoration of damaged and degraded stream sections will be required as well as work at a watershed scale. Where are the best possibilities for restoration, what is required to accomplish this, and what will this cost? Who will undertake these herculean tasks? Should this have started long before now?

Multiple cumulative effects assessments done in cutthroat watersheds tell a similar and graphic tale – the future of cutthroat (and other native trout) persistence is at risk because of the land-use footprint, which is large and growing. That is the elephant in the room (or in the watershed). Habitat issues from land use are interlinked and cannot be separated from those of harvest and hybridization. Dealing with the fires of harvest and hybridization, getting them under control, is essential. Failure to grapple with land use will potentially compromise all the other efforts.

The biggest challenge is to ensure westslope cutthroat trout population recovery proceeds at a pace faster than losses and that habitats are secured and protected before they disappear. If that doesn't happen, the fate of the species will mirror that of my grandfather's pocket watch – the hands frozen in place when the time ran out for repairs.

## NOAH AND THE FISH
### A Lesson for Our Times

Occasionally, when rain becomes a downpour, I think of the reported biblical flood and the first major biodiversity conservation initiative. I speak, of course, of Noah's efforts recorded in Genesis, to collect a minimum of two of everything and save them from that apocalyptic, spiritually cleansing flood.

What concerns me about this apocryphal tale is the apparent biodiversity bigotry, if not rampant species racism, of the first conservation effort. Noah took "clean beasts, and beasts not so clean, and of fowls and of everything that creepeth upon the earth." The instructions were specific to "everything on the dry land in whose nostrils was the breath of life." God's goal was clear, "Every living substance that I have made will I destroy from off the face of the earth." In summary, this was to be a clean sweep of his creation. Anything missing on the gang plank to the ark, you might ask?

There is stunning silence in this biblical tale about fish and other aquatic creatures. Similarly, there is no reference to plants, except for the olive leaf brought back eventually by a dove. Presumably a 150-day period of inundation would have been enough to do in most plants. That an olive tree survived extended flooding is a miracle in its own right. The Bible is mute on the effect of the flood duration on fish, but it seems axiomatic that they survived, maybe even prospered with new territory to exploit.

Maybe fish were originally revered as righteous creatures, not requiring divine protection from the cleansing flood. If that were true, the ancient perspective and respect has been lost. But fish and plants don't "creep," as in the original instructions, and so it seems to me they were overlooked. This is the condition that persists into modern times.

Biodiversity conservation has smacked of the Noah syndrome ever since, largely ignoring aquatic creatures and plants. Because of this, species in these groups are the most critically imperilled provincially, nationally and globally. Noah wasn't an ecologist; he was a carpenter, so it really isn't his fault. Noah didn't know, but that first conservation effort set the stage for others in failing to understand and implement initiatives to maintain all biodiversity. Not just the critters that run, jump, fly and breathe air on dry land – the charismatic megafauna – but everything.

The ones that swim, take root and extract oxygen in other ways need the same attention and publicity Noah gave the terrestrial animals. In Alberta we have imperilled populations of bull trout and westslope cutthroat trout. Over most of their range the classification of the current status of these species might be termed "extinguished." To some extent people might recognize the term "trout." The reality is that most people couldn't tell a trout from a fish stick, let alone understand the relevance of the St. Mary sculpin, another fish species in short supply. Most people are woefully ignorant of fish species – their presence, biology, importance, distribution and status.

Grizzly bears have hogged the endangered species spotlight, with good reason. But when you mention tiny cryptanthe, the response is "tiny what?" Porsid's bryum will evoke a wrinkled brow and western spiderwort will have the listener's eyes glaze over. Short of the few botanists in this country, many of us couldn't distinguish these plants from pansies, or celery.

Ironically, we are more conversant with introduced garden-variety plants than the native ones that define our landscapes. About 12,000 years of rough fescue growth gave us the black soils that sparked the development of the province and still sustain agriculture. Only belatedly, after most of it disappeared, did we confer upon it the designation of "Provincial" grass.

Even that produced some inspired snickering, mostly from the benches in the Alberta legislature, about other "grass," the non-native one that is typically inhaled. Sadly, most of the species in dire straits are the uncharismatic microfauna, or flora – too small, too unseen, too cryptic or too localized to be recognized and appreciated.

This is especially true for fish, living largely out of our sight in a world alien to us terrestrial creatures. It is just beginning to dawn on us that fish are important indicators of the health of our world. A world, I might add, that is 70 per cent water –

so much so we should have called it "Aqua," not "Earth." As Earthlings, living on dry land, we have given short shrift to our finned neighbours.

The closest many of us get to fish is when we take them out of a package and eat them; globally we have been eating them at an astonishing and unsustainable pace. Many of the rest we are squeezing out of their place with our ever-increasing footprint. We are not of their world, yet everything we do affects theirs. We terrestrial, air-breathing humans have never really got our minds around fish, although our jaws are around them frequently.

This speaks to a key task of ecologists, biologists, educators and resource managers – creating awareness among the public, politicians and industry of these species. A little bit of ecological literacy about plants and fish would go a long ways to creating a greater constituency that knows about, cares about and values all biodiversity. I will know we have "made it" when a plant or a fish gets top billing in people's minds as an item of biodiversity concern. A new and large generation of "fern feelers" and "fish squeezers" is desperately required.

Although jam-packed, the original ark could only have been partially filled with Earth's biodiversity treasures. The perhaps metaphorical flood story gives the mistaken impression that these treasures, the life on earth (but not in the water), could be easily gathered up and housed in a small place. The delusion continues in our thinking that a few scattered parks and protected areas will suffice to conserve biodiversity. As a pathway to future inclusiveness, it would be helpful to understand and acknowledge these significant biblical oversights and how, perhaps subconsciously, they have influenced past conservation efforts.

The ark story needs a rewrite with an update! Today's ark (otherwise known as Earth) can ill afford to ignore any species. Otherwise, we build our conservation initiatives on a great story but an old one with poor ecological thinking. The original story is found in Genesis; we now need the genesis of a new awareness and inclusiveness for the conservation of all species.

# Epilogue

———

*The future isn't a place that we're going to go,
it's a place that you get to create.*

—Nancy Duarte

Since I have more years behind me than ahead of me, I am persuaded to think more about the future, the one beyond me. Although the past has some nostalgic elements to it, as Mark Twain observed, "The older I get, the more clearly I remember things that never happened." I have become more focused on an intrusive, contemplative and compelling question that we all should ask ourselves: When we pass from this life, what will we leave behind?

The answer to this question becomes the starting point to a commitment to being a good ancestor, someone unwilling to impose harm or unwarranted risk to future people. Marian Wright Edelman, a civil rights activist, said of this, "Be a good ancestor. Stand for something bigger than yourself. Add value to the Earth during your sojourn."

This appeals to me since I don't want the children of the future cursing me, a ghost from their past, for limiting their opportunities and security. As Kevin Van Tighem, conservationist and nature writer, says, "One hits a fulcrum in life where one transitions from being a descendent and starts worrying about being a good ancestor."

This might start with self-awareness, not self-indulgence. Ellen Meloy, a nature writer, remarked, "Stay curious. Know where you are – your biological address. Get to know your neighbors – plants, creatures, who lives there, who died there, who is blessed, cursed, what is absent or in danger or in need of your help. Pay attention to the weather, to what breaks your heart, to what lifts your heart. Write it down." Articulating these things makes it easier to communicate with others, to encourage them to look deeply at what is important as a legacy.

Each of us is just one link in a chain that passes from yesterday into tomorrow. Like one definition of stewardship, which is people planting trees they know they will never sit in the shade of, our lives and accomplishments are transitory. The way we make them meaningful is to ensure we pass the torch to others and ensure it is lit.

Very rarely do big things get done in one generation – it takes several. It's also a question of scale. Climate change is a huge elephant, and as a hunter friend wisely points out, "It takes a big gun to shoot an elephant." Positive outcomes (and personal rewards) may well happen after we're gone. But what's important is that progress was made, and we had a hand in that achievement.

I hope the answer to what we leave behind isn't a bunch of unnecessary stuff, a feature of over-consumption. "We have multiplied our possessions, but reduced our values," wisely intones

Bob Moorehead, author of *Words Aptly Spoken*. Our consumer culture is killing the Earth – colonizing the future – leaving future generations powerless, unable to protect themselves.

We would be well advised to fall back to the old mantra of reuse it, wear it out, make it do and do without. It's not painless; it takes resolve, but we use less of Earth's resources in the process. If we were more fixated on the full cost of stuff, beyond the price tag, we might become more conscious consumers. If we were to wean ourselves of defining our lives by stuff, the Earth would benefit. As a bonus, the next generation isn't stuck sifting through our stuff, trying to figure out what to do with it.

Traditional societies venerated their elders because they were repositories of experience and wisdom. A generation is seldom given enough power to foresee the lingering effects of its labour, but there are always a few survivors who, at the end of their lives, have a chance to look back over their shoulders at what has been gained or lost. They are worth listening to, for it affords the opportunity to avoid past mistakes and to build on successful decisions.

The best, most valuable bequests for our children include teaching them critical thinking skills, the ability to use information to make wise decisions, and leaving a quality environment in which there are still opportunities and choices to make. To hold ourselves accountable for acting like better ancestors, we'd be wise to encourage young people to be more vocal about what matters and to question the way things are done. We should listen to youth at every opportunity, around dinner and conference tables. When we exercise our vote in elections and invest in companies, the interests of the youngest living generation need to be at the top of our priority lists.

I know it's hard to get beyond the immediacy of today – finishing up a project, remembering to fill the car with gas, and contemplating dinner. Today stretches into the near future, to an upcoming and much-anticipated vacation. But contemplating paying off the mortgage is just so far into a vague tomorrow it seems unreachable. That's the dilemma of thinking about and planning for the future – it just seems so far off.

Our descendants own the future, but the decisions and actions we make now will tremendously impact generations to come. As John W. Dafoe, a Canadian journalist, noted, "It would be well to bear in mind that the present of today was the future of yesterday and that it is what it is because of the human actions, the human decisions of yesterday. Therefore, the future will be what we make it."

Even though we build the future every day, imagining it eludes us. We think we cannot plan well for something we cannot see, especially the future. The greatest discovery in each generation is that we can alter the future by changing what we do today. Instead of treating the future as an abstraction, we can use factual knowledge to allow an informed choice to be made about tomorrow's options.

As a pathway to a sustainable future, thought, planning and foresight allow today's decisions to be measured against tomorrow's realities. Then we can start to answer the question: How do we imagine the future and what do we want it to be? Hopefully, the answer centres around a quality environment.

In the annals of shipwrecks there is always the cautionary tale of those who drowned trying to take their gold with them. Apparently, gold is not a good life preserver. Modern life has been made so easy, so convenient and so unbearably comfortable we lose track of what really counts. Each of us has choices to make. Maintaining healthy ecosystems and restoring damaged ones are clear choices. Alternately, we could blindly accept the temporary fruits of using up, abusing or neglecting the things that actually support us.

How about an investment in the things that assure us (and generations to come) of fresh air to breath, fresh water to drink, fertile soil, biodiversity and ecological integrity? That would be a life jacket for subsequent generations (and our own) rather than starter castles, adult toys and investment portfolios.

For societies, it's never been more important to think ahead to future generations. A meaningful way to give to the future is to think bigger and leave behind something that can be stewarded – and used and adapted over time – as a legacy. Don Ruzicka, a land steward, has an additional element in the recipe: "You have to put something in if you want something back." This also means leaving behind resources with an eye to how they might endure for multiple generations, without prescribing too narrowly what each generation does with them.

It would serve subsequent generations well if we acted like tenants of the Earth and renters of its resources, not owners with a penchant for exploiting everything in our time here. Each generation borrows from the next and should remember that any debts accrued will fall to the next group.

Hilton Pharis, a foothills rancher, once confided in me that he wanted to leave his ranch better than he found it. I thought, this could only come from someone profoundly aware of his responsibility to others. To do that the Pharis family committed to lessening the footprint of grazing, fixing the damaged landscape bits and living within the constraints of the land. The goal was to bequeath the land to the next generation, as Hilton's generation had been given it, and possibly in better shape.

This is inspirational – live lightly, do little harm, make do with less and leave it as you found it, maybe better. It seems like a starting formula for a good ancestor's Hippocratic oath.

# Acknowledgements

A book does not spring forth, fully formed. It develops organically, with the help and suggestions of many. I'd like to acknowledge Ian Urquhart, Barry Adams, Richard Schneider, Connie Simmons, Andrew Hurly, Michael Sullivan, Peter Kingsmill, Kirby Smith and the late Hugh Wollis for their thoughtful suggestions, editorial comments and attempts to keep me honest. The illustrations that grace each chapter represent the artistic talent of Liz Saunders, Sandpiper Ecological Research and Illustrations.

Writing *Travels Up the Creek* was easy – all that was required was opening up a vein in my arm and letting the content pour out on the pages. This is only partly metaphorical. There is no artificial intelligence in the book, only scar tissue. It is scar tissue shared with so many of my biologist colleagues over years of resource conflicts and very few victories.

What I learned from those colleagues was some days you have to work hard to save a river, a forest or a trout. Some days the river, the forest and the trout save you.

What saves me every day is the support of my wife, Cheryl Bradley.

# About the Author

**Lorne Fitch** has been a biologist for over 50 years, working mostly in Alberta but also in other parts of Canada and with some international experience. He has criss-crossed the province, learned the landscape, investigated fish and wildlife populations, and engaged with ranchers, farmers, industry, and bureaucrats over conservation. His insights are the result of much scar tissue.

He is a professional biologist, a retired provincial fish and wildlife biologist, and a former adjunct professor with the University of Calgary. He is also the co-founder of the riparian stewardship initiative Cows & Fish.

For his work on conservation he has been part of three Alberta Emerald awards, an Alberta Order of the Bighorn award and a Canadian Environment Gold Award, with additional recognition from the Wildlife Society, the Society for Range Management, the Alberta Society of Professional Biologists, the Western Association of Fish and Wildlife Agencies, and the Alberta Wilderness Association.

His first book with RMB was *Streams of Consequence: Dispatches from the Conservation World*. Lorne lives in Lethbridge, Alberta.